The everyday world at your fingertips

PICTURE DICTIONARY
JAPANESE

www.berlitzpublishing.com

Distribution

UK, Ireland and Europe:
Apa Publications (UK) Ltd;
sales@insightguides.com

United States and Canada:
Ingram Publisher Services;
ips@ ingramcontent.com

Australia and New Zealand:
Woodslane; info@ woodslane.com.au

Southeast Asia:
Apa Publications (SN) Pte;
singaporeoffice@insightguides.com

Worldwide: Apa Publications (UK) Ltd;
sales@insightguides.com

**Special Sales, Content Licensing
and CoPublishing**

Insight Guides can be purchased in bulk
quantities at discounted prices. We can
create special editions, personalised
jackets and corporate imprints tailored to
your needs. sales@insightguides.com;
www.insightguides.biz

First Edition 2019

Contact us

Every effort has been made to provide
accurate information in this publication,
but changes are inevitable. The publisher
cannot be responsible for any resulting
loss, inconvenience or injury. We would
appreciate it if readers would call our
attention to any errors or outdated
information. We also welcome your
suggestions; please contact us at: berlitz@
apaguide.co.uk

Series Editor: Carine Tracanelli
Editor: Urszula Krajewska
Head of Production: Rebeka Davies
Series design: Krzysztof Kop
Picture research & DTP design:
bookidea
English text: Carine Tracanelli &
Barbara Marchwica
Translation & simplified phonetics:
Aligua
Photo credits: all Shutterstock and
Fotolia

Introduction

Whether you are a total beginner or already have a sound knowledge of your chosen language, this Berlitz picture dictionary will help you to communicate quickly and easily. Packed with 2,000 useful terms, it covers all everyday situations, whether you're applying for a job, going shopping or just getting around. See, understand, memorise: visual learning by combining a word with an image helps you remember it more effectively as images affect us more than text alone.

To get the most out of your picture dictionary you can search for words in two ways: by theme (women's clothes, sporting facilities, hobbies, etc.) or by consulting the index at the end. You'll also find important phrases surrounding a topic in each chapter, ensuring that you have the foundations you need for communicating.

Each word is followed by its phonetic transcription to ensure you pronounce each word or sentence correctly. You will find a guide to pronunciation in your chosen language on pages 7–10. Note that the terms in this picture dictionary are always given in their singular form unless they are generally only used in their plural form. Certain terms are not gender neutral and in such cases all genders are provided in both the translation and phonetic transcription, so you can communicate in all variants.

Berlitz are renowned for the quality and expertise of their language products. Discover the full range at www.berlitzpublishing.com.

Table of Contents

Pronunciation

Compared to other languages, the Japanese alphabet has a relatively small amount of sounds, with only 14 consonants (k, s, t, n, h, m, y, r, w, g, z, d, b, p) and 5 vowels (a, e, i, o, u). In Japanese there are no words with three or more consonants together in a row. The Japanese language is composed of syllables, which comprise of a consonant and a vowel. The only exceptions are the vowels and the sound 'n', which is on its own.

When it comes to word order, Japanese follows the formula of SOV (Subject, Object, Verb).

The Japanese language relies not on one but three different alphabets. These are hiragana, katakana and kanji.

Hiragana: The hiragana syllabary is composed of 46 symbols, each one representing a different sound. Each hiragana symbol derives from the cursive writing of certain kanji ideograms that, with the passage of time, were simplified to represent a single sound. Hiragana is used to write mostly all the inflections and modifications of verbs, adjectives, adverbs and particles.

Katakana: Like hiragana, the katakana syllabary also consists of 46 sounds. The symbols are different, but the sounds they represent are exactly the same as hiragana. The use of katakana was originally useful for Buddhist monks in making pronunciation notations and comments on the lessons and teaching of the sacred scriptures of Buddhism. Currently the use of katakana is used almost exclusively to write words of foreign origin.

Kanji: Are ideograms of Chinese origin that were introduced in Japan around the 4th century.

This group of characters is used mainly to write the root of verbs, adjectives, some adverbs, nouns and the proper names of people and places.

This section is designed to make you familiar with the sounds of Japanese by using the romanised version of Japanese words (using Latin script to write the Japanese language). There are several different romanisation systems. The system used in this dictionary is Kunrei-shiki romanisation (ISO 3602). Simply follow the roman letter to pronounce the words correctly.

Hiragana	Katakana	Roman letter	Pronunciation	Example
あ	ア	A	AH	father
い	イ	I	EE	meet
う	ウ	U	OO	boot
え	エ	E	EH	met
お	オ	O	OH	boat
や	ヤ	YA	YAH	yard
ゆ	ュ	YU	YOO	you
よ	ヨ	YO	YOH	yore
か	カ	KA	KAH	cause
き	キ	KI	KEE	key
く	ク	KU	KOO	cool
け	ケ	KE	KEH	ketchup
こ	コ	KO	KOH	coat

さ	サ	SA	SAH	saw
し	シ	SHI	SHEE	she
す	ス	SU	SOO	Sue
せ	セ	SE	SEH	set
そ	ソ	SO	SOH	so
た	タ	TA	TAH	tall
ち	チ	CHI	CHEE	cheat
つ	ツ	TSU	TSOO	tsunami
て	テ	TE	TEH	tell
と	ト	TO	TOH	toe
な	ナ	NA	NAH	not
に	ニ	NI	NEE	knee
ぬ	ヌ	NU	NOO	new
ね	ネ	NE	NEH	net
の	ノ	NO	NOH	no
は	ハ	HA	HAH	hunt
ひ	ヒ	HI	HEE	head
ふ	フ	FU	FOO	fu or hu
へ	ヘ	HE	HEH	head
ほ	ホ	HO	HOH	hoe
ま	マ	MA	MAH	mall
み	ミ	MI	MEE	me
む	ム	MU	MOO	mood
め	メ	ME	MEH	met
も	モ	MO	MOH	most
や	ヤ	YA	YAH	yacht
ゆ	ユ	YU	YOO	you
よ	ヨ	YO	YOH	yoke
ら	ラ	RA	RAH	rush
り	リ	RI	REE	reel

る	ル	RU	ROO	roof
れ	レ	RE	REH	review
ろ	ロ	RO	ROH	role
を	ヲ	WO	WOH	walk
ん	ン	N	N	n
が	ガ	GA	GAH	gap
ぎ	ギ	GI	GEE	geese
ぐ	グ	GU	GOO	good
げ	ゲ	GE	GEH	get
ご	ゴ	GO	GOH	got
ざ	ザ	ZA	ZAH	zap
じ	ジ	JI	JEE	jeers
ず	ズ	ZU	ZOO	zoom
ぜ	ゼ	ZE	ZEH	zest
ぞ	ゾ	ZO	ZOH	zone
だ	ダ	DA	DAH	dunk
ぢ	チ	DZI	JEE	jeez
づ	ヅ	DZU	DZOO	zoo
で	デ	DE	DEH	date
ど	ド	DO	DOH	dog
ば	バ	BA	BAH	back
び	ビ	BI	BEE	beer
ぶ	ブ	BU	BOO	book
べ	ベ	BE	BEH	bay
ぼ	ボ	BO	BOH	bottom
ぱ	パ	PA	PAH	pass
ぴ	ピ	PI	PEE	peel
ぷ	プ	PU	POO	poor
ぺ	ペ	PE	PEH	pending
ぽ	ポ	PO	POH	potential

GENERAL VOCABULARY

first name
名前
Nahmah-eh

last name
名字
MEE-o-jee

date of birth
生年月日
Seh-ee-nen khappee

age
年齢
Nen-reh-ee

place of birth
出身地
SHOOH-sheen-chee

email address
電子メールアドレス
Denshee-mehroo

phone number
電話番号
DEHwha-bankho

REGISTRATION FORM

Applying For A   (Check any that apply)
☐ Permit   ☐ ID Card   ☐ Renewal   ☐ Replacement

Your Personal
Full Last Name
Full First Name
Date of birth ___/___/___   Gender ☐ Male ☐ Female
Place of birth   Age

Identification Information
Driver license?   ☐ Yes ☐ No
Learner permit?   ☐ Yes ☐ No
Non-driver ID Card?   ☐ Yes ☐ No

PHOTO HERE

ID card number and Details
_____ enter the identification number it appears on the card
Date of Expiration: Type of License: Out-of-State License ID No:

Your Personal Details
Hight ___ /___   Eye color _____
Email Address: (optional)
Status: ☐ Single ☐ Married ☐ Devorced
Others

Contact Details
Home Phone No.
Mobile Phone No.
Fax No.   Work

Address where you live
Unit No.   Street No.   Street
Town/City   State   Post Code
Country

Address where you get your mail
(This address will appear on your document)
Has your mailing address changed?   ☐ Yes
Other change: (new license class, wrong date of birth, etc.)?
What is the change and the reason for it

Social security number (SSN)*
☐☐☐-☐☐-☐☐☐☐

1. Do you wear glasses or contact lenses?   ☐ Yes ☐ No
2. Do you have a physical or mental condition which requires that you take medication?   ☐ Yes ☐ No
3. Have you ever had a seizure, blackout , or loss of consciousness?   ☐ Yes ☐ No
4. Do you have a physical condition which requires you to use special equipment in order to work?   ☐ Yes ☐ No
5. Have you ever had a seizure, blackout , or loss of consciousness?   ☐ Yes ☐ No
6. Have you been convicted within the past ten years in this state or elsewhere of any offense   ☐ Yes ☐ No
7. Have you resulting from your operation of, or involving , a motor vehicle?   ☐ Yes ☐ No

address	住所	YOOH-shoh
marital status	配偶者の有無	KHA-EE khushah no oomoo
children	子供	Kohdohmoh
home country	国籍	Kohkuh-she-kee
place of residence	住居	ee-JYoo
single	独身	Doh-ku-sheen
in a relationship	交際中	Kohsaee-chuh
divorced	離婚	RiKONH
married	既婚	Kee-KOhn
widowed	寡婦	KAH-foo
What's your name?	あなたの名前はなんですか。	Ahnahtah no nahmaeh wa nanhdesukah
Where are you from?	出身はどこですか。	SHUhheen wa dohkoh desukah
Where were you born?	どこで生まれましたか。	Dohkoh deh oomarehmashitah kah
When were you born?	生年月日を教えてください	Seh-ee-nehn-gahp-pee Woh Oh-shee-eh-teh Koo-dah-sah-ee
What is your address?	住所を教えて下さい。	YOOshoh wo oshee-ehteh koodasaee
What's your phone number?	電話番号を教えて下さい。	DehNwah bangoh wo ohsee-ehteh koodahsaee
Are you married?	既婚者ですか。	Kee-Kohn shah des kah
Do you have children?	子供はいますか。	Kohdohmoh wa eemas kah

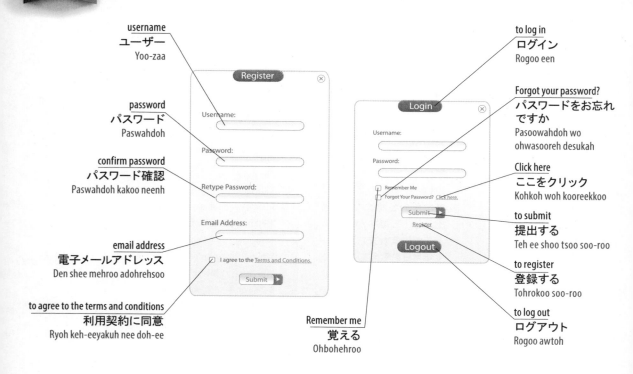

username
ユーザー
Yoo-zaa

password
パスワード
Paswahdoh

confirm password
パスワード確認
Paswahdoh kakoo neenh

email address
電子メールアドレス
Den shee mehroo adohrehsoo

to agree to the terms and conditions
利用契約に同意
Ryoh keh-eeyakuh nee doh-ee

Register

Username:

Password:

Retype Password:

Email Address:

☑ I agree to the Terms and Conditions.

Submit ▶

to log in
ログイン
Rogoo een

Forgot your password?
パスワードをお忘れ
ですか
Pasoowahdoh wo
ohwasooreh desukah

Click here
ここをクリック
Kohkoh woh kooreekkoo

to submit
提出する
Teh ee shoo tsoo soo-roo

to register
登録する
Tohrokoo soo-roo

to log out
ログアウト
Rogoo awtoh

Login

Username:

Password:

☐ Remember Me
☐ Forgot Your Password? Click here.

Submit ▶
Register

Logout

Remember me
覚える
Ohbohehroo

0 1 2 3 4 5 6 7 8 9

0	zero	ゼロ	Zeroh		17	seventeen	十七	Jyoo nahnah
1	one	一	Eechee		18	eighteen	十八	Jyoo khachee
2	two	二	Nee		19	nineteen	十九	Jyoo kyoo
3	three	三	San		20	twenty	二十	Nee jyoo
4	four	四	Yon / shee		21	twenty-one	二十一	Nee jyoo eechee
5	five	五	Goh		30	thirty	三十	San jyoo
6	six	六	Rohkoo		40	forty	四十	Yon jyoo
7	seven	七	Nahnah / Sheechee		50	fifty	五十	Goh jyoo
8	eight	八	Khachee		60	sixty	六十	Rohkoo jyoo
9	nine	九	Kyoo		70	seventy	七十	Nahnah jyoo
10	ten	十	Jyoo		80	eighty	八十	Khachee jyoo
11	eleven	十一	Jyoo eechee		90	ninety	九十	Kyoo jyoo
12	twelve	十二	Jyoo nee		100	one hundred	百	Kheeahkoo
13	thirteen	十三	Jyoo san		101	one hundred and one	百一	Kheeahkoo eechee
14	fourteen	十四	Jyoo yon		1000	one thousand	千	Sen
15	fifteen	十五	Jyoo goh		1 000 000	one million	百万	Kheeakoo man
16	sixteen	十六	Jyoo rohkoo					

1ST (FIRST)
第一
Dahee eechee

2nd (second)		3rd (third)	
第二		第三	
Dahee nee		Dahee san	

4th	fourth	第四	Dahee yon
5th	fifth	第五	Dahee goh
6th	sixth	第六	Dahee rohkoo
7th	seventh	第七	Dahee nahnah
8th	eighth	第八	Dahee khachee
9th	ninth	第九	Dahee kyoo
10th	tenth	第十	Dahee jyoo
11th	eleventh	第十一	Dahee jyoo eechee

12th	twelfth	第十二	Dahee jyoo nee
13th	thirteenth	第十三	Dahee jyoo san
14th	fourteenth	第十四	Dahee jyoo yon
15th	fifteenth	第十五	Dahee jyoo goh
16th	sixteenth	第十六	Dahee jyoo rohkoo
17th	seventeenth	第十七	Dahee jyoo nahnah
18th	eighteenth	第十八	Dahee khachee
19th	nineteenth	第十九	Dahee jyoo kyoo
20th	twentieth	第二十	Dahee nee jyoo
21st	twenty-first	第二十一	Dahee nee jyoo eechee
22nd	twenty-second	第二十二	Dahee nee jyoo nee
23rd	twenty-third	第二十三	Dahee nee jyoo san
24th	twenty-fourth	第二十四	Dahee nee jyoo yon
25th	twenty-fifth	第二十五	Dahee nee jyoo goh
26th	twenty-sixth	第二十六	Dahee nee jyoo rohkoo
27th	twenty-seventh	第二十七	Dahee nee jyoo nahnah
28th	twenty-eighth	第二十八	Dahee nee jyoo khachee
29th	twenty-ninth	第二十九	Dahee nee jyoo kyoo
30th	thirtieth	第三十	Dahee san jyoo
40th	fortieth	第四十	Dahee yonn jyoo
50th	fiftieth	第五十	Dahee goh jyoo
60th	sixtieth	第六十	Dahee rohkoo jyoo
70th	seventieth	第七十	Dahee nahnah jyoo
80th	eightieth	第八十	Dahee khachee jyoo
90th	ninetieth	第九十	Dahee kyoo jyoo
100th	hundredth	第百	Dahee kheeakoo

noon	正午	Shohgoh
midnight	真夜中	Mahyohnahkah

one am	午前1時	Gohzen eecheegee
one pm	午後1時	Gohgoh eecheegee

two am	午前2時	Gohzen neegee
two pm	午後2時	Gohgoh neegee

three am	午前3時	Gohzen san gee
three pm	午後3時	Gohgoh san gee

four am	午前4時	Gohzen yoh gee
four pm	午後4時	Gohgoh yoh gee

five am	午前5時	Gohzen goh gee
five pm	午後5時	Gohgoh goh ge

six am	午前6時	Gohzen rohkoogee
six pm	午後6時	Gohgoh rohkoogee

seven am	午前7時	Gohzen nahnah gee
seven pm	午後7時	Gohgoh nahnah gee

eight am	午前8時	Gohzen khachee gee
eight pm	午後8時	Gohgoh khachee gee

nine am	午前9時	Gohzen koogee
nine pm	午後9時	Gohgoh koogee

ten am	午前10時	Gohzen jyoo gee
ten pm	午後10時	Gohgoh jyoo gee

eleven am	午前11時	Gohzen jyoo eechee gee
eleven pm	午後11時	Gohgoh jyoo eechee gee

quarter to
○ ○ ○ 15分前
... Jyoo goh foon mah-eh

ten to
○ ○ ○ 10分前
Jyoo poon mah-eh

five to
○ ○ ○ 5分前
... Goh fun mah-eh

... o'clock
○ ○ ○ 時
... Gee

five past
○ ○ ○ 5分
... Goh foon

ten past
○ ○ ○ 10分
... Jyoo poon

quarter past
○ ○ ○ 15分
... Jyoo goh fun

half past
○ ○ ○ 半
... Khan

What time is it?	何時ですか。	Nahn gee des kah
It's nine thirty.	9時30分です。	Koo gee san jyoo poon des
Excuse me, could you tell me the time please?	すみません、時間を教えてくれませんか。	Soo-meemahsen, gee-kahn wo ohshee-ehteh koo-dah-sah-ee
It's about half past nine.	9時半くらいです。	Koo gee Hahn koo-rah-ee des

Monday
月曜日
Geh-tsoo yoh-bee

Tuesday
火曜日
Kah yoh-bee

Wednesday
水曜日
Soo-ee yoh-bee

Thursday
木曜日
Moh-koo yoh-bee

Friday
金曜日
Keen yoh-bee

Saturday
土曜日
Doh yoh-bee

Sunday
日曜日
Neechee yoh-bee

on Monday	月曜日に	Geh-tsoo yoh-bee nee
from Tuesday	火曜日から	Kah yoh-bee nee
until Wednesday	水曜日まで	Soo-ee yoh-bee mah-deh

JANUARY	FEBRUARY	MARCH	APRIL
January	February	March	April
一月	二月	三月	四月
Eechee gah-tsoo	Nee gah-tsoo	San gah-tsoo	Shee gah-tsoo

MAY	JUNE	JULY	AUGUST
May	June	July	August
五月	六月	七月	八月
Goh gah-tsoo	Roh-koo gah-tsoo	Shee-chee gah-tsoo	Kha-chee gah-tsoo

SEPTEMBER	OCTOBER	NOVEMBER	DECEMBER
September	October	November	December
九月	十月	十一月	十二月
Kyoo gah-tsoo	Jyoo gah-tsoo	Jyoo ee-chee gah-tsoo	Jyoo nee gah-tsoo

in July	7月に	Shee-chee ga-tsoo
since September	9月から	Koo ga-tsoo
until October	10月まで	Jyoo ga-tsoo mahdeh
for two months	二ヶ月間	Nee kah geh-tsoo kahn

morning	late morning	noon	afternoon	evening	night
朝	**昼前**	**正午**	**午後**	**夕方**	**夜**
Ah-sah	Khee-roo mah-eh	Shoh-goh	Goh-goh	Yoo-gah-tah	Yoh-roo

in the morning	午前中に	Goh sehn choo nee
in the evening	夕方に	Yoo-gah-tah nee
in the night	夜に	Yoh-roo nee

cash
現金
Gehn-keen

ATM / cashpoint
ATM
Eh-tee-ehmoo

bank statement
口座明細証
Koh-za meh-ee-saee shoh

cheque
小切手
Koh-khee-tteh

account	口座	Koh-za
bank	銀行	Kheen-koh
bank charges	銀行手数料	Kheen-koh the-soo-ryoh
debit card	デビットカード	Deh-beettoh kah-doh
debt	借金	Shah-kkeen
current account	当座預金	Toh-za yoh-keen
loan	ローン	Roh-ohn
mortgage	住宅ローン	Gyoo-tahkoo roh-ohn
savings account	普通預金口座	Foo-tsoo yoh-keen koh-za
standing order	講座自動振替	Koh-za gee-doh foo-ree kah-eh
to borrow money	お金を借りる	Oh-kaneh wo kah-ree-roo
to invest	投資する	Toh-shee soo-roo
to lend money	資金を貸す	Shee-keen wo kah-soo
to pay	支払う	Shee-khah-rah-oo
to take out a loan	ローンを組む。	Roh-ohn wo koo-moo
to withdraw from the account	講座から引き出す。	Koh-za kahrah khikee-dah-soo
to take out a mortgage	住宅ローンを組む。	Gyoo-tahkoo roh-ohn wo koo-moo
to withdraw	引き出し	Khee-kee dah-shee

credit card
クレジットカード
Koo-reh-gee-ttoh kahdoh

to save
貯金する
Choh-keen soo-roo

Pound Sterling
ポンド
Pohn-doh

Euro
ユーロ
Yoo-roh

Dollar
ドル
Doh-roo

Franc
フランク
Foo-rahn-koo

Yen
円
Ehn

Won
ウオン
Oo-ohn

Yuan
元
Khehn

Indian Rupee
ルピー
Roo-pee

Zloty
ズウォティ
Zoo-who-tee

Ruble
ルーブル
Roo-boo-roo

Leu
レウ
Reh-oo

Forint
フォリント
Foh-ren-toh

Krone	クローネ	Koo-roh-neh
Peso	ペソ	Peh-soh
Pound	ポンド	Pohn-doh
Dinar	ディナール	Dee-nah-roo
Shilling	シリング	Shee-reen-goo
Dirham	ディルハム	Dee-roo-kha-moo
Rial	リアル	Ree-ah-roo
Dong	ドン	Dohn

exchange rate	両替レート	Ryoh-khaeh reh-toh
exchange rate for US Dollars to Japanese Yen	米ドルから日本円の両替レート	Beh-ee doh-roo kahrah Nee-khohn noh Ryoh-khaeh reh-toh
foreign exchange	外貨	Khaee-kah
foreign exchange rate	外貨の両替レート	Khaee-kah noh Ryoh-khaeh reh-toh

 PEOPLE

a middle-aged man
中年の男性
Choo-nehn noh dahn-she-ee

an old man
老人
Roh-jeen

a young man
若者
Wah-kah-mohnoh

a young woman
若い女性
Wahkah-ee jyoh-seh-ee

baby
赤ちゃん
Ak-kah-chahn

a teenage boy
十代の男性
Jyoo-dahee noh dahn-seh-ee

a young boy
若い男子
Wahkah-ee danhn-shee

a teenage girl
十代の女子
Jyoo-dah-ee noh jyoh-shee

teenager	十代の人	Jyoo-dah-ee noh khee-toh
a young girl	若い女子	Wahkah-ee jyoh-shee
a seven-year-old girl	7歳の少女	Nahnah-sah-ee noh shoh-jyoh
young	若い	Wahkah-ee
middle-aged	中年	Choo-nehn
old	年寄り	Toh-shee toh-ree
adult	大人	Oh-toh-nah
She is forty years old.	彼女は４０歳です。	Kah-noh-jyoh wa jyohn-jyoo sah-ee des
She is in her thirties.	彼女は３０代です。	Kah-noh-jyoh wah sahn-jyoo dah-ee des
She is about twenty.	彼女は２０歳くらいです。	Kah-noh-jyoh wah kha-tah-chee koorah-ee des
child	子供	Koh-doh-moh
a little boy	男の子	Ohtohkoh noh koh
a little girl	女の子	Ohn-nah noh koh
He is six years old.	彼は6歳です。	Kah-reh wah rok-koo sah-ee des

a beautiful girl
美しい女性
Oo-tsoo-koo-shee jyoh-she-ee

a pretty woman
美しい女性
Oo-tsoo-koo-shee jyoh-seh-ee

a handsome man
かっこいい男
Kah-kkoh-ee oh-toh-koh

attractive	魅力的	Mee-ryoh-koo teh-kee		dirty	汚い	Kee-tah-nah-ee
beautiful	美しい	Oo-tsoo-koo-shee		elegant	上品	Jyoh-kheen
cute	可愛い	Kah-wah-ee		pretty	可愛い	Kah-wah-ee
handsome	かっこいい	Kah-kkoh-ee		fashionable	おしゃれ	Oh-shah-reh
ugly	醜い	Mee-nee-koo-ee		neat	清潔	Se
unattractive	魅力的ではない	Mee-ryoh-koo the-kee deh wah nah-ee		poorly dressed	貧相な服装	Kheen-soh nah foo-koo-soh
casually dressed	カジュアルな服装	Kah-jyooah-roo nah foo-koo-soh		untidy	控えめ	Khee-kah-eh-meh
				well-dressed	おしゃれ	Oh-shah-reh

27

She is taller than him.	彼女は彼より背が高い。	Kah-noh-jyoh wah kah-reh yohree she gah tah-kah-ee
He isn't as tall as her.	彼は彼女ほど背が高くない。	Kah-reh wah kah-noh-jyo khohdoh she gah tah-kah-koo-nah-ee
She is of average height.	彼女の身長は平均的です。	Kahnoh-jyo noh sheehn-choh wah kheh-keen-tehkee des

very tall
とても背が高い
Toh-the-moh she gah tah-kah-ee

tall
背が高い
She khah tah-kah-ee

quite tall
かなり背が高い
Kah-nah-ree she gah tah-kah-ee

not very tall
そんなに背が高くない
Sohn-nah-nee she gah tah-kah-koo-nah-ee

short
背が低い
She gah khee-koo-ee

thin
細い
Khoh-soh-ee

slim
スリム
Soo-ree-moo

plump
ふくよか
Foo-koo-toh-kah

fat
太い
Foo-toh-ee

slender	細身	Hohsoh-mee
skinny	痩せてる	Yahseh-teh-roo
obese	肥満	Khee-mahn
underweight	痩せすぎ	Yah-seh-soo-gee
overweight	太り過ぎ	Foo-toh-ree-soo-gee
She is overweight / underweight.	彼女は太り過ぎです。・痩せすぎです	Kahnoh-jyo wah foo-toh-ree-soo-gee / Yah-seh-soo-gee
to lose weight	痩せる	Yahseh-roo

grey
白髪
Dhee-rah-gah

red
赤髪
Ah-kah-gah-mee

dark
ダークヘア
Dah-koo khe-ah

black
黒髪
Koo-roh kah-mee

blond
金髪
Keen-pah-tsoo

light
明るい
Ah-kah-roo-ee

chestnut
ライトブラウン
Rah-ee-toh boo-rah-uhn

brown
茶色
Chah-ee-roh

straight
ストレート
Soo-toh-reh-toh

curly
パーマ
Pah-mah

wavy
ウエーブ
Weh-boo

thick
太い髪
Foo-toh-ee kah-mee

bald
毛のない
Keh noh nah-ee

long
ロングヘア
Rohn-goo khe-ah

short
ショートヘア
Shoh-toh khe-ah

shoulder-length
肩まで
Kah-tah mah-deh

medium-length
ミディアムロング
Mee-dee-ahmoo khe-ah

a brunette	ブルネットの	Booroo-neh-ttoh
a redhead	赤髪の	Ah-ka gah-mee noh
a blonde	金髪の	Keen-pahtsoo noh
a dark-haired woman	黒髪の女性	Koo-roh kah-mee noh jyoh-seh-ee
He has long dark hair.	彼は長くて黒い髪がある。	Kahreh wa nah-gah-koo-teh koo-roh-ee kamee gah ah-roo
He has curly hair.	彼はパーマがかかってる 。	Kahreh wah pah-mah gah kahkah-tteh-roo
He is bald.	彼は髪の毛がない。	Kahreh wah kahmee no keh gah nah-ee

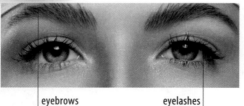

eyebrows	eyelashes
眉毛	睫毛
Mah-yoo-kheh	Mah-tsoo-kheh

glasses
メガネ
Meh-gah-neh

sunglasses
サングラス
Sahn-goo-rah-soo

blue	青色	Ah-oh-ee-roh
grey	グレー	Goo-reh
green	緑色	Mee-doh-ree ee-roh
brown	茶色	Chah-ee-roh
dark	黒い	Koo-roh-ee
light	ライト	Rah-ee-toh

short sighted	近視	Keen-shee
blind	盲目	Moh-mohkoo
She wears glasses.	彼女はメガネかけいます。	Kah-noh-jyoh wah meh-gah-neh kah-keh-the-ee-mas
She has blue eyes.	彼女の目は青いです。	Kahnoh-jyoh noh meh wah ah-oh-ee des
His eyes are dark brown.	彼の目はダークブラウンです。	Kahreh noh meh wah dah-koo boo-rah-oon des

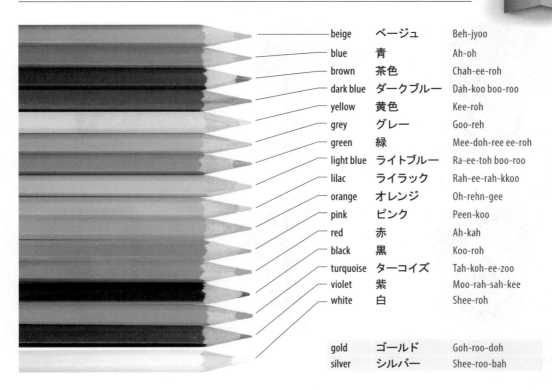

beige	ベージュ	Beh-jyoo
blue	青	Ah-oh
brown	茶色	Chah-ee-roh
dark blue	ダークブルー	Dah-koo boo-roo
yellow	黄色	Kee-roh
grey	グレー	Goo-reh
green	緑	Mee-doh-ree ee-roh
light blue	ライトブルー	Ra-ee-toh boo-roo
lilac	ライラック	Rah-ee-rah-kkoo
orange	オレンジ	Oh-rehn-gee
pink	ピンク	Peen-koo
red	赤	Ah-kah
black	黒	Koo-roh
turquoise	ターコイズ	Tah-koh-ee-zoo
violet	紫	Moo-rah-sah-kee
white	白	Shee-roh

| gold | ゴールド | Goh-roo-doh |
| silver | シルバー | Shee-roo-bah |

positive
前向き
Mah-eh-moo-kee

stubborn
頑固
Gahn-koh

lucky
ラッキー
Rah-kkee

dreamer
夢想家
Yoo-soh-ka

visionary
空想家
Koo-soh-kah

funny
面白い
Oh-moh-shee-roh-ee

talkative
おしゃべり
Oh-shah-beh-ree

energetic
活動的
Kah-tsoo-doh-the-kee

negative
ネガティブ
Neh-gah-tee-boo

creative	クリエイティブ	Kooree-ey-tee-boo
adventurous	冒険者	Boh-kehn-shah
kind	親切	Sheen-she-tsoo
calm	穏やかな	Ohdah-yah-kah-nah
caring	愛情深い	Ah-ee-jyoh-boo-kah-ee
punctual	時間を守る	Gee-kahn woh mah-moh-roo
crazy	クレージー	Ku-reh-gee
liar	嘘つき	Oo-soh-tsoo-kee
frank	正直	Shoh-gee-kee
strong	強い	Tsoo-yoh-ee

family
家族
Kah-zoh-koo

aunt
おばさん
Oh-bah-sahn

uncle
おじさん
Oh-gee-sahn

grandparents
祖父母
Soh-foo-boh

parents
両親
Ryoh-sheen

sister-in-law (older sister)
義理のお姉さん
Gee-ree noh ohneh-sahn

sister-in-law (younger)
義理の妹
Gee-ree noh ee-moh-toh

sister
姉妹
Shee-mah-ee

cousin
いとこ
Ee-toh-koh

brother
兄弟
Kyoh-dah-ee

nephew
甥っ子
Oh-ee-kkoh

niece
姪っ子
Meh-ee-kkoh

myself
私
Wah-tah-shee

wife
妻
Tsoo-mah

grandchildren	孫	Mah-goh
daughter	娘	Moo-soo-meh
father	お父さん	Otoh-sahn
father-in-law	義理のお父さん	Gee-ree noh otoh-sahn
grandchild	孫	Mah-goh
granddaughter	孫娘	Mah-goh moo-soo-meh
grandfather	お祖父さん	Oh-gee-sahn
grandmother	お祖母さん	Oh-bah-sahn
grandson	孫息子	Mah-goh moo-soo-koh
great-grandparents	曽祖父母	Soh-sohfoo-boh
husband	夫	Oh-ttoh
mother	お母さん	Oh-kah-sahn
mother-in-law	義理のお母さん	Gee-ree noh oh-kah-sahn
son	息子	Moo-soo-koh
twin brother	双子	Foo-tah-goh
brother-in-law (Older brother)	義理のお兄さん	Gee-ree noh oh-nee-sahn
brother-in-law (younger brother)	義理の弟	Gee-ree noh oh-toh-toh

single child
一人っ子
Khee-tohree-kkoh

family with two children
二児を持つ家族
Nee-gee who moh-tsoo kah-zoh-koo

big family
大家族
Oh-kah-zoh-koo

childless
子供なし
Koh-doh-moh nahshee

single father
シングルファーザー
Sheen-goo-roo fah-zah

single mother
シングルマザー
Sheen-goo-roo mah-zah

adoption
養子縁組
Yoh-shee-ehn-goo-mee

orphan
孤児
Mee-nah-shee-goh

widow
未亡人
Mee-boh-jeen

stepfather	義父	Gee-foo
stepmother	継母	Gee-boh
to be pregnant	妊娠する	Neen-sheen soo-roo
to expect a baby	赤ちゃんを待つ	Ah-kah-chahn who mah-tsoo
to give birth to	出産する	Shoo-sahn soo-roo
born	産む	Uh-muh
to baptise	洗礼を受ける	Sehn-reh-ee woh oo-keh-roo
to raise	育てる	Soh-dah-the-roo

to be engaged	婚約	Kohn-yahkoo
to marry	結婚する	Keh-kkohn soo-roo
to be married to	結婚しています	Keh-kkohn shee-the-eemahs
divorced	離婚	Ree-kohn
widowed	寡婦	Kah-foo
widower	男やもめ	Oh-to-koh yah-moh-meh
to die	死ぬ	Shee-noo

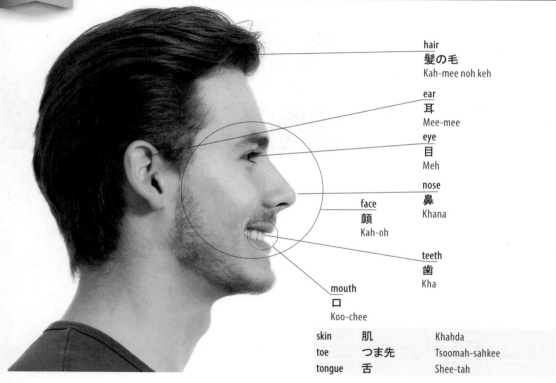

hair
髪の毛
Kah-mee noh keh

ear
耳
Mee-mee

eye
目
Meh

nose
鼻
Khana

face
顔
Kah-oh

teeth
歯
Kha

mouth
口
Koo-chee

skin	肌	Khahda
toe	つま先	Tsoomah-sahkee
tongue	舌	Shee-tah

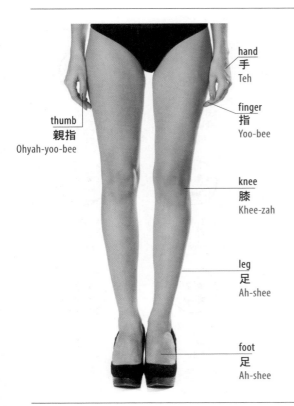

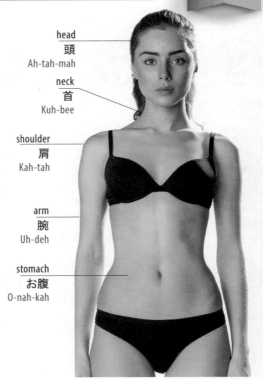

hand
手
Teh

thumb
親指
Ohyah-yoo-bee

finger
指
Yoo-bee

knee
膝
Khee-zah

leg
足
Ah-shee

foot
足
Ah-shee

head
頭
Ah-tah-mah

neck
首
Kuh-bee

shoulder
肩
Kah-tah

arm
腕
Uh-deh

stomach
お腹
O-nah-kah

angry
怒る
Oh-koh-roo

annoyed
迷惑
Meh-ee-wah-koo

ashamed
恥ずかしい
Kha-zoo-ka-shee

betrayed
裏切られる
Oo-rah-gee-rah-reh-roo

confused
混乱する
Kohn-rahn soo-roo

confident
自信
Jee-sheen

cheated
騙される
Dah-mah-sah-reh-roo

depressed
落ち込む
Oh-chee-koh-moo

delighted
喜ぶ
Yoh-roh-koh-boo

disappointed
がっかりする
Gah-kkaree-soo-roo

excited
興奮する
Koh-foohn soo-roo

embarrassed
恥ずかしい
Kha-zoo-kah-shee

furious
激怒する
Geh-kee-doh

frightened
恐る
Oh-soh-reh-roo

happy
嬉しい
Oo-reh-shee

horrified
恐ろしがる
Ohsohrohshee-gahroo

irritated
苛立つ
Eerah-dah-tsoo

intrigued
興味を持つ
Kee-ohmee who moh-tsoo

jealous
嫉妬する
Shee-ttoh soo-roo

lazy
だるい
Dah-roo-ee

lucky
ラッキー
Rah-kkee

relaxed
くつろぐ
Koo-tsoo-roh-goo

sad
悲しい
Kah-nah-shee

stressed
ストレス
Soo-toh-reh-soo

terrified
怖がる
Koh-wah-gah-roo

upset
動揺
Doh-Yoh

unhappy
不幸
Foo-koh

hobby	My hobby is . . .	私の趣味は。。。	Wah-tah-shee noh shoo-mee wah . . .
趣味	Are you interested in . . . ?	。。。に興味ありますか。	. . . nee kyoh-mee ah-ree-mahs-kah
Shoo-mee			

baking
ベーキング
Beh-keen-goo

coin collecting
コイン集め
Koh-een ah-tsoo-meh

woodworking
木工
Moh-koh

stamp collecting
切手集め
Kee-tteh ahtsoo-meh

cooking
料理
Ryo-ree

dance
踊る
Oh-doh-roo

drawing
スケッチ
Soo-keh-tchee

reading
読書
Doh-koo-shoh

jewellery making
ジュエリー作り
Joo-eh-ree tsoo-koo-ree

knitting
編み物
Ah-mee-moh-noh

painting
絵を描く
Eh who kah-koo

sewing
縫い物
Noo-ee-moh-noh

badminton
バドミントン
Bah-doh-meen-toh

bowling
ボーリング
Boh-reen-goo

boxing
ボクシング
Boh-koo-sheen-goo

chess
チェス
Cheh-soo

cycling
サイクリング
Sah-ee-koo-reen-goo

darts
ダーツ
Dah-tsoo

diving
ダイビング
Dah-ee-been-goo

fishing
釣り
Tsoo-ree

football
サッカー
Sah-kkah

orienteering
オリエンテーリング
Ohree-ehn-the-reen-goo

gymnastics
体操
Tah-ee-soh

handball
ハンドボール
Khahn-doh-boh-roo

jogging
ジョギング
Jyo-geen-goo

kayaking
カヤック
Kah-yah-kkoo

martial arts
格闘技
Kah-kootoh-gee

mountain biking
マウンテンバイク
Mah-oon-teh-een ba-ee-koo

paintball
ペイントボール
Peh-een-toh boh-roo

photography
写真
Shah-sheen

47

rock climbing
ロッククライミング
Roh-kkoo koo-rah-ee-meen-goo

running
ランニング
Rahn-neen-goo

sailing
セーリング
She-reen-goo

surfing
サーフィング
Sah-feen-goo

swimming
水泳
Soo-ee-eh

table tennis
卓球
Tahk-kyoo

travel
旅行
Ryoh-koh

tennis
テニス
Te-nee-soo

yoga
ヨガ
Yoh-gah

I like to swim.	私は泳ぐのが好きです。	Wah-tah-shee wah oh-yoh-goo noh gah soo-kee dehs
What activities do you like to do?	どのようなアクティビティーがしたいですか	Doh-noh yoh-nah ah-koo-tee-bee-tee gah shee-tah-ee dehs kah

to get up
起きる
Oh-kee-roo

to take a shower
シャワーを浴びる
Shah-wah who ah-bee-roo

to brush your teeth
歯を磨く
Kha who mee-gah-koo

to floss your teeth
フロスする
Foo-roh-su soo-roo

to shave
髭を剃る
Khee-geh who soh-roo

to brush your hair
髪をとかす
Kah-mee who toh-kah-soo

to put on makeup
化粧をする
Keh-shoh who soo-roo

to get dressed
服を着る
Foo-koo who kee-roo

to get undressed
服を脱ぐ
Foo-koo who noo-goo

to take a bath
お風呂に入る
Ofoo-roh nee kha-ee-roo

to go to bed
寝る
Neh-roo

to sleep
寝る
Neh-roo

Valentine's Day
バレンタインデー
Bah-rehn-ta-ee deh

graduation
卒業
Soh-tsoo-gyoh

Easter
イースター
Ee-soo-tah

engagement
婚約
Kohn-yahkoo

marriage
結婚
Keh-kkohn

bride
花嫁
Khana-yohmeh

Christmas
クリスマス
Koo-ree-soo-mah-soo

Santa Claus / Father Christmas
サンタクロース
Sahn-tah koo-roh-soo

candle
キャンドル
Kyahn-doh-roo

decoration
飾り付け
Kah-zah-ree tsoo-keh

mistletoe
宿り木
Yah-doh-ree-gee

present / gift
プレゼント
Poo-reh-sehn-toh

champagne
シャンパーニュ
Shahn-pah-nyuh

fireworks
花火
Khana-bee

Advent calendar
アドベントカレンダー
Ah-doh-behntoh kah-rehn-dah

party
パーティー
Pah-tee

birthday
誕生日
Than-jyoh-bee

ceremony
セレモニー
She-reh-moh-nee

wedding ring
結婚指輪
Keh-kkohn yoo-bee-wah

decorated eggs
イースターの卵
Ee-soo-tah noh tah-mah-goh

Easter Bunny
イースターうさぎ
Ee-soo-tah oo-sah-gee

New Year	新年	Sheen-nehn
Happy New Year!	明けましておめでとう御座います	Ah-keh-mah-shee-teh
Happy Birthday!	誕生日おめでとうございます	Than-jyoh-bee oh-meh-deh-toh goh-zay-mah-soo
All the best!	成功を祈ります	She-koh who ee-noh-ree-mahs

Congratulations!	おめでとうございます	Oh-meh-deh-toh goh-za-ee-mas
Good luck!	頑張ってください	Gahn-bah-tteh koo-dah-sah-ee
Merry Christmas!	メリークリスマス	Meh-ree koo-re-mahs
Happy Easter!	ハッピーイースター	Khah-ppee ee-soo-tah

Christianity
キリスト教
Kee-ree-soo-toh kyoh

Confucianism
儒教
Jyuh-kyoh

Jainism
ジャイナ教
Jah-ee-nah kyoh

Islam
イスラム教
Ee-soo-rah-moo kyoh

Buddhism
仏教
Boo-kkyoh

Judaism
ユダヤ教
Yoo-dah-yah kyoh

Hinduism
ヒンドゥー教
Kheen-doo kyoh

Taoism
道教
Doh-kyoh

Sikhism
シーク教
Shee-koo kyoh

to confess	懺悔	Zahn-geh
without religious confession	無宗教	Moo-shoo-kyoh
to believe in God	神様を信じる	Kah-mee-sah-mah woh sheen-gee-roo
to have faith	信仰を持つ	Sheen-kyoh woh mo-tsoo
to pray	お祈りする	Oh-ee-noh-ree soo-roo

 HOME & HOUSEKEEPING

house
家
Ee-eh

flat
アパート
Ah-pah-toh

block of flats
マンション
Mahn-shohn

duplex / two-storey house
二階屋
Nee-kah-ee-yah

detached house
一軒家
Ee-kkehn-yah

co-ownership
共用所有
Kyoh-yoh-shoh-yoo

houseboat
ハウスボート
Khah-oo-soo boh-toh

caravan
キャラバン
Kyah-rah-bahn

farm
牧場
Boh-koo-jyoh

flatshare
共有アパート
Kyoh-yoo ah-pah-toh

Where do you live?	どこに住んでいますか。	Doh-koh nee soon-deh-ee-mahs-kah
I live in a flatshare.	私は共有アパートに住んでいます。	Wah-tah-see wah kyoh-yoo ah-pah-toh nee soon-deh-ee-mahs
I live with my parents.	両親と住んでいます。	Ryoh-sheen toh soon-deh-ee-mas

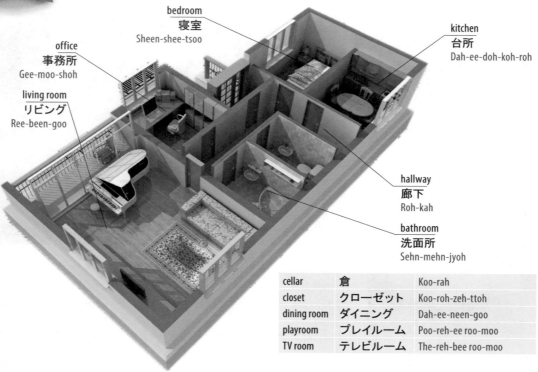

bedroom
寝室
Sheen-shee-tsoo

kitchen
台所
Dah-ee-doh-koh-roh

office
事務所
Gee-moo-shoh

living room
リビング
Ree-been-goo

hallway
廊下
Roh-kah

bathroom
洗面所
Sehn-mehn-jyoh

cellar	倉	Koo-rah
closet	クローゼット	Koo-roh-zeh-ttoh
dining room	ダイニング	Dah-ee-neen-goo
playroom	プレイルーム	Poo-reh-ee roo-moo
TV room	テレビルーム	The-reh-bee roo-moo

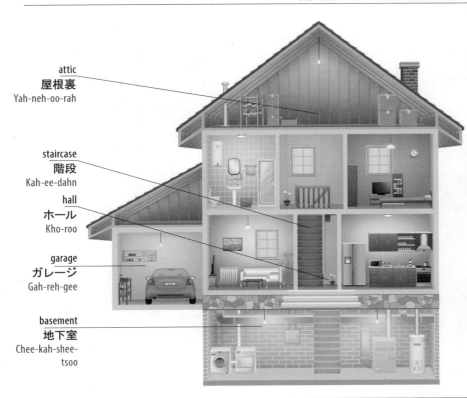

attic
屋根裏
Yah-neh-oo-rah

staircase
階段
Kah-ee-dahn

hall
ホール
Kho-roo

garage
ガレージ
Gah-reh-gee

basement
地下室
Chee-kah-shee-
tsoo

porch
玄関
Khehn-kahn

patio
パティオ
Pah-tee-oh

workshop
作業場
Sah-gyoh-bah

59

window
窓
Mah-doh

bed
ベッド
Beh-ttoh

lamp
ランプ
Rahn-poo

pillow
まくら
Mah-koo-rah

chest of drawers
箪笥
Than-soo

blanket
ブランケット
Boo-rahn-keh-ttoh

bedsheet
シーツ
Shee-tsoo

carpet
カーペット
Kah-peh-ttoh

bedroom
寝室
Sheen-shee-tsoo

bed linen   リネン   Ree-nehn

bathroom
洗面場
Sehn-mehn-jyoh

toilet
トイレ
To-ee-reh

bidet
ビデ
Bee-deh

mirror
鏡
Kah-gah-mee

shower
シャワー
Shah-wah

tap
蛇口
Gyah-goo-chee

bath towel
バスタオル
Bah-soo tah-oh-roo

wash basin
洗面器
Sehn-mehn-kee

bath
お風呂
Oh-foo-roh

flush
便器
Behn-kee

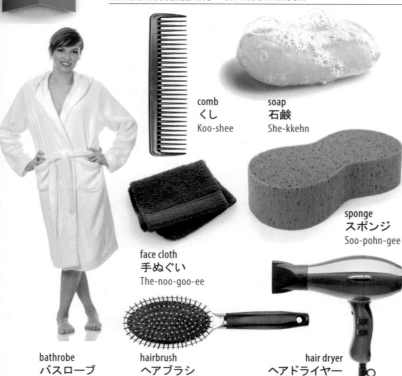

comb
くし
Koo-shee

soap
石鹸
She-kkehn

dental floss
糸ようじ
Ee-toh yoh-gee

sponge
スポンジ
Soo-pohn-gee

rubbish bin
ゴミ箱
Goh-mee bah-koh

face cloth
手ぬぐい
The-noo-goo-ee

bathrobe
バスローブ
Bah-soo roh-boo

hairbrush
ヘアブラシ
Heh-ah boo-rah-shee

hair dryer
ヘアドライヤー
Heh-ah doh-rah-ee-yah

hand towel
ハンドタオル
Hahn-doh tah-oh-roo

towel
タオル
Tah-oh-roo

shaving cream
シェービングクリーム
Sheh-been koo-ree-moo

toothbrush
歯ブラシ
Hah boo-rah-shee

razor
髭剃り
Khee-geh-soh-ree

shampoo
シャンプー
Shahn-poo

toothpaste
歯磨き
Hah-mee-gah-kee

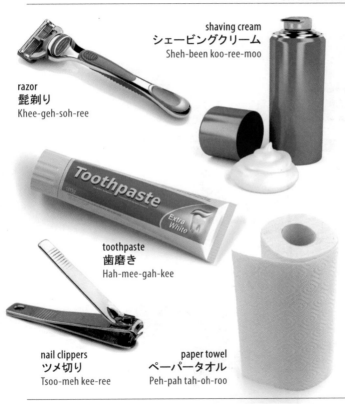

conditioner
コンディショナー
Kohn-dee-shoh-nah

nail clippers
ツメ切り
Tsoo-meh kee-ree

paper towel
ペーパータオル
Peh-pah tah-oh-roo

toilet paper
トイレットペーパー
Toh-ee-reh-ttoh peh-pah

microwave
電子レンジ
Dehn-shee rehn-gee

fridge
冷蔵庫
Reh-ee-zoh-koh

stove
レンジ
Rehn-gee

coffee machine
コーヒーマシン
Koh-hee mah-sheen

dishwasher
食器洗い機
Shoh-kkee ah-rah-ee kee

freezer
冷凍庫
Reh-toh-koh

washing machine
洗濯機
Zehn-tah-koo-kee

oven
オーブン
Oh-boon

kettle
ケトル
Keh-roo-toh

toaster
トースター
Toh-soo-tah

cookery book
料理本
Ryoh-ree bohn

dishcloth
ふきん
Foo-keen

draining board
排水器
Ha-ee-soo-ee-kee

kitchen roll
キッチンロール
keet-cheen roh-roo

plug
栓
Sehn

tea towel
ティータオル
Tee tah-oh-roo

shelf
棚
Tah-nah

sink
流し台
Nah-gah-shee da-ee

tablecloth
テーブルクロス
The-boo-roo Koo-roh-soo

bottle opener
栓抜き
Sehn-noo-kee

chopping board
まな板
Mah-nah ee-tah

colander
ざる
Zah-roo

frying pan
フライパン
Foo-rah-ee pahn

grater
おろし金
Oh-roh-shee gah-neh

juicer
ジューサー
Jyoo-sah

corkscrew
コルク抜き
Koh-roo-koo noo-kee

kitchen scales
キッチンスケール
Keet-cheen soo-keh-roo

mixing bowl
ミキシングボウル
Mee-kee-sheen-goo boh-oo-roo

sieve
ざる
Zah-roo

saucepan
鍋
Nah-beh

whisk
泡立て器
Ah-wah tah-the kee

tin opener
缶切り
Kahn-kee-ree

washing-up liquid
洗浄液
Sehn-jyoh-eh-kee

to do the dishes / to do the washing up	食器を洗う	Shohk-kee who ah-rah-oo
to do the washing	洗濯をする。	Sah-rah ah-rah-ee woh soo-roo
to clear the table	テーブルを拭く	The-boo-roo woh foo-koo
to set the table	テーブルをセットする	The-boo-roo woh seht-toh soo-roo

cutlery	食器	Shohk-kee
dessert spoon	デザートスプーン	Deh-zah-toh Soo-poon
soup spoon	スープスプーン	Soo-poo soo-poon
spoon	スプーン	Soo-poon

tablespoon
大さじ
Oh-sah-gee

fork
フォーク
Foh-koo

knife
ナイフ
Nah-ee-foo

teaspoon
ティースプーン
Tee-soo-poon

coffee spoon
コーヒースプーン
Kph-hee soo-poon

plate
お皿
Oh-sah-rah

mug
マグカップ
Mah-goo kahp-poo

sugar dispenser
砂糖ディスペンサー
Sah-toh dee-soo-pehn-sah

jug
ジャグ
Jyah-goo

saucer
受け皿
Oo-keh-zah-rah

cup
カップ
Kahp-poo

wine glass
ワイングラス
Wah-een goo-rah-soo

teapot
ティーポット
Tee poht-toh

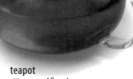

bowl
ボウル
Boh-oo-roo

jar
ビン
Been

crockery	食器	Shohk-kee
glass	グラス	Goo-rah-soo

69

armchair
アームチェア
Ah-moo cheh-ah

sofa
ソファー
Soh-fah

lampshade
ランプシェード
Rahn-poo sheh-doh

lamp
ランプ
Rahn-poo

vase
花瓶
Kah-been

rug
じゅうたん
Jyoo-tahn

bookcase
本棚
Hohn-dah-nah

shelf
棚
Tah-nah

plant
植物
Shoh-koo-boo-tsoo

picture
絵画
Kah-ee-gah

table
テーブル
The-boo-roo

chair
椅子
Ee-soo

I can relax here.	ここでリラックスできる。	Koh-koh deh ree-rahk-koo-soo deh-kee-roo
Do you watch TV often?	あなたはよくテレビ見ますか。	Ah-nah-tah wah yoh-koo the-reh-bee mee-mahs kah
What is the size of the living room?	リビングルームのサイズは？	Ree-been-goo roo-moo noh sah-ee-zoo wah?

hair dryer
ヘアードライヤー
Heh-ah doh-rah-ee-yah

iron
アイロン
Ah-ee-rohn

washing machine
洗濯機
Sehn-tah-koo-kee

radio
ラジオ
Rah-gee-ohr

television
テレビ
The-reh-bee

telephone
電話機
Denh-wah kee

cooker
コンロ
Kohn-roh

vacuum cleaner
掃除機
Soh-gee-kee

mobile
携帯電話
Keh-tah-ee dehn-wah

microwave
電子レンジ
Dehn-shee rehn-gee

kettle
やかん
Yah-kahn

refrigerator
冷蔵庫
Reh-zoh-koh

coffee grinder
コーヒ挽き
Koh-hee hee-kee

sewing machine
ミシン
Mee-sheen

razor
髭剃り
Hee-geh-soh-ree

blender
ブレンダー
Boo-rehn-dah

mixer
ミキサー
Mee-kee-sah

gas stove
ガスコンロ
Gah-soo kohn-roh

juicer
ジューサー
Jyoo-sah

73

to dust
ホコリを取る。
Hoh-koh-ree woh toh-roo

to vacuum
掃除機をかける。
Soh-gee-kee woh kah-keh-roo

to clean the windows
窓を拭く。
Mah-doh woh foo-koo

to clean the floor
床掃除をする。
Yoo-kah soh-gee woh soo-roo

to wash the clothes
服を洗う
Foo-koo Woh A-rah-oo

to do the dishes
皿洗いをする。
Sah-rah ah-rah-ee woh soo-roo

to clean up
掃除をする。
Soh-gee woh soo-roo

to make the bed
ベッドを用意する。
Beht-doh woh yoh-ee soo-roo

to hang up the laundry
洗濯物を干す。
Sehn-tah-koo moh-noh woh
hoh-soo

to iron
アイロンをかける。
Ah-ee-rohn woh kah-keh-roo

bucket
バケツ
Bah-keh-tsoo

dust cloth
ぞうきん
Zoh-keen

feather duster
羽ぼうき
Hah-neh boh-kee

mop
モップ
Mohp-poo

broom
ほうき
Hoh-kee

dustpan
ちり取り
Chee-ree-toh-ree

clothes line
物干し
Moh-noh hoh-shee

peg
洗濯バサミ
Sehn-tah-koo bah-sah-mee

paper towel
ペーパータオル
Peh-pah tah-oh-roo

laundry basket
洗濯カゴ
Sehn-tah-koo kah-goh

scrubbing brush
たわし
Tah-wah-shee

window cleaner
窓クリーナー
Mah-doh koo-ree-nah

sponge
スポンジ
Soo-pohn-gee

detergent
洗剤
Sehn-za-ee

We have to clean up.	掃除する必要があります。	Soh-gee soo-roo hee-tsoo-yoh gah ah-ree-mah-soo.
The flat is already clean.	アパートはもうきれいです。	Ah-pah-toh wah moh kee-reh-ee dehs
Who does the cleaning?	誰が掃除しましたか。	Dah-reh gah soh-gee shee-mah-shee-tah kah

LESSONS

 SCHOOL

white board
ホワイトボード
Hoh-ah-ee-toh
boh-doh

chair
椅子
Ee-soo

book
本
Hohn

table
机
Tsoo-koo-eh

clock
時計
Toh-keh-ee

teacher
先生
Sehn-she-ee

student
生徒
She-ee-toh

tablet
タブレット
Tah-boo-reht-toh

calculator
電卓
Dehn-tah-koo

to go to school	学校に行く	Gahk-koh nee ee-koo		marks	点数	Tehn-soo
to study	勉強する	Behn-kyoh soo-roo		an oral exam	口頭試験	Koh-toh shee-kehn
to learn	学ぶ	Mah-nah-boo		a written exam	筆記試験	Heek-kee shee-kehn
to do homework	宿題をする	Shoo-koo-dah-ee soo-roo		to prepare for an exam	試験の準備をする	Shee-kehn noh jyoon-bee woh soo-roo
to know	知る	Shee-roo				
to take an exam	試験を受ける	Sheee-kehn woh oo-keh-roo		to repeat a year	留年	Ryoo-nehn
to pass	合格	Goh-kah-koo				

Languages
言語
Gehn-goh

 Spanish
スペイン語
Soo-peh-een goh

 German
ドイツ語
Doh-ee-tsoo goh

 English
英語
Eh-ee goh

 French
フランス語
Foo-rahn-soo goh

Art
美術
Bee-jyoo-tsoo

Geography
地理
Chee-ree

Music
音楽
Ohn-gah-koo

History
歴史
Reh-kee-shee

Chemistry
化学
Kah-gah-koo

Biology
生物
She-ee-boo-tsoo

Mathematics
数学
Soo-gah-koo

Physical education
体育
Tah-ee-koo

scissors
ハサミ
Hah-sah-mee

globe
地球儀
Chee-kyoo-gee

school bag
学生カバン
Gah-koo-seh-ee
kah-bahn

pen
ペン
Pehn

notebook
ノート
Noh-toh

pencil case
筆箱
Foo-deh-bah-koh

ruler
定規
Jyoh-gee

pencil
鉛筆
Ehn-pee-tsoo

pencil sharpener
鉛筆削り
Ehn-pee-tsoo
keh-zoo-ree

rubber
消しゴム
Keh-shee-goh-moo

highlighter
蛍光ペン
Keh-ee-koh pehn

book
本
Hohn

colouring pen
カラーペン
Kah-rah pehn

stapler
ホッチキス
Hoht-chee-kee-soo

WORK

job interview
面接
Mehn-seh-tsoo

recruiter
リクルーター
Ree-koo-roo-tah

candidate
志望者
Shee-boh-shah

CV
履歴書
Ree-reh-kee-shoh

application letter
志望理由書
Shee-boh-ree-yoo-shoh

gross	税込み	Zeh-ee-koh-mee		interview	インタビュー	Eehn-tah-byoo
net	税抜き	Zeh-ee-noo-kee		job	仕事	Shee-goh-toh
job advertisement	求人広告	Kyoo-jeehn koh-koh-koo		salary	給料	Kyoo-ryoh
application	申し込み	Moh-shee-koh-mee		vacancy	欠員	Keh-tsoo-eehn
company	会社	Kah-ee-shah		work	作業	Sah-gyoh
education	教育	Kyo-ee-koo		to hire	雇う	Yah-toh-oo

experience	経験	Keh-ee-kehn
to apply for	申し込む	Moh-shee-koh-moo
assessment	評価	Hyoh-kah
bonus	ボーナス	Boh-nah-soo
employer	雇用者	Koh-yoh-sha
to fire	クビにする	Koo-bee nee soo-roo
fringe benefits	フリンジベネフィット	Fee-reehn-gee beh-neh-feet-toh
maternity leave	産休	Sahn-kyoo
notice	通知	Tsoo-chee
staff	スタッフ	Soo-tahf-foo
human resource officer	人事担当者	Jeehn-jee than-toh-sha
promotion	出世	Shoos-seh-ee
prospects	見込み	Mee-koh-mee
to resign	辞職する	Jee-shoh-koo soo-roo
to retire	引退する	Eehn-tah-ee soo-roo
sick leave	病欠	Byoh-keh-tsoo
strike	ストライキ	Soo-toh-rah-ee-kee
trainee	研修生	Kehn-shoo-seh-ee
training course	研修	Kehn-shoo
unemployment benefits	退職金	Tah-ee-shoh-koo-keehn
workplace	職場	Shooh-koo-bah

employee
従業員
Jyoo-gyoh-eehn

actor
役者
Yah-koo-sha

baker
パン職人
Pahn-shoh-koo-neehn

banker
銀行員
Geehn-koh-eehn

butcher
肉屋
Nee-koo-yah

carpenter
大工
Dah-ee-koo

chef
料理人
Ryo-ree-neehn

doctor
医者
Ee-shah

farmer
農家
Noh-kah

fisherman
漁師
Gyoh-shee

firefighter
消防士
Shoh-boh-shee

musician
音楽家
Ohn-gah-koo-kah

lawyer
弁護士
Behn-goh-shee

nurse
看護師
Kahn-goh-shee

pilot
パイロット
Pah-ee-roht-toh

policeman
警察官
Keh-ee-sah-tsoo-kahn

coach
コーチ
Koh-chee

sailor
船乗り
Foo-nah-noh-ree

soldier
兵士
Heh-ee-shee

teacher
先生
Sehn-se-ee

judge
審判
Sheehn-pahn

tailor
仕立て職人
Shee-tah-the
shoh-koo-neehn

veterinarian
獣医
Jyoo-ee

waiter
ウェイター
Oo-eh-tah

mechanic
整備士
Seh-ee-bee-shee

accountant	会計士	Kah-ee-keh-shee
barber	理容師	Ree-yoh-shee
beautician	美容師	Bee-yoh-shee
broker	ブローカー	Boo-roh-kah
driver	運転手	Oohn-tehn-shoo
craftsman	職人	Shoh=koo=neehn
dentist	歯医者	Ha-ee-shah
engineer	エンジニア	Ehn-jee-nee-ah
pharmacist	薬剤師	Yah-koo-za-ee-shee
writer	作家	Sahk-kah
politician	政治家	Seh-jee-kah
professor	教授	Kyoh-joo
salesman	セールスマン	Seh-roo-soo-mahn
shoemaker	靴職人	Koo-tsoo-shoh-koo-neehn
watchmaker	時計職人	Toh-keh-ee-shoh-koo-neehn
What's your occupation?	あなたのご職業は？	Ah-nah-tah noh shoh-koo-gyoh wah?
I work as a secretary.	秘書として働いています。	Hee-shoh toh-shee-the hah-tah-rah-ee-teh-ee-mah-soo
I am a teacher.	私は教師です。	Wah-tah-shee wah kyo-shee-des

desk
デスク
Deh-soo-koo

office
事務所
Jee-moo-shoh

computer
コンピューター
Kohn-pyoo-tah

drawer
引き出し
Hee-kee-dah-shee

printer
プリンター
Poo-reehn-tah

filing cabinet
ファイリングキャビネット
Fah-ee-reehn-goo kya-bee-neht-toh

rubber stamp
ゴム印
Goh-moo-jee-roo-shee

telephone
電話
Dehn-wah

ink pad
インクパッド
Eehn-koo-pahk-koo

bin
チリ箱
Chee-ree-bah-koh

swivel chair
回転椅子
Kah-ee-tehn-ee-ee-soo

keyboard
キーボード
Kee-boh-doh

clipboard	クリップボード	Koo-reehp-poo-boh-doh
file	ファイル	Fah-ee-roo
in-tray	イントレイ	Eehn-toh-reh-ee
to photocopy	コピーする	Koh-pee-soo-roo
to print	印刷する	Eehn-sah-tsoo-soo-roo

bulldog clip
クリップ
Koo-reep-poo

calculator
電卓
Dehn-tah-koo

correction tape
修正テープ
Shoo-seh-ee-the-poo

envelope
封筒
Foo-toh

laptop
ラップトップ
Rahp-poo-tohp-poo

highlighter
蛍光ペン
Keh-koh-pehn

letterhead
レターヘッド
Retah-heht-toh

holepunch
パンチ
Pahn-chee

elastic bands
ゴムバンド
Goh-moo-bahn-doh

notepad
メモ帳
Meh-moh-choh

pen
ペン
Pehn

pencil sharpener
鉛筆削り
Ehn-pee-tsoo-keh-zoo-ree

paper clip
ペーパークリップ
Peh-pah-koo-reep-poo

personal organiser
個人用整理手帳
Koh-jeehn-seh-ree-the-choh

pencil
鉛筆
Ehn-pee-tsoo

sticky tape
粘着テープ
Nehn-chah-koo-the-poo

stapler
ホッチキス
Hoht-chee-kee-soo

staples
ホッチキスの芯
Hoht-chee-kee-soo-noh-sheehn

 FOOD AND DRINK

apple juice
りんごジュース
Reehn-goh-jyoo-soo

grapefruit juice
グレープフルー
ツジュース
Goo-reh-poo-foo-
roo-tsoo-jyoo-soo

orange juice
オレンジジュ
ース
Orehn-jee-jyoo-
soo

tomato juice
トマトジュース
Toh-mah-toh-jyoo-soo

coffee
コーヒー
Koh-hee

milk
牛乳
Gyoo-nyoo

tea
お茶
Oh-chah

with lemon
レモン入り
Reh-mohn-ee-ree

water
水
Mee-zoo

| with milk | ミルク入り | Mee-roo-koo-ee-ree | decaffeinated | ノンカフェイン | Nohn-kah-feh-eehn |
| black | ブラックコーヒー | Boo-rahk-koo-koh-hee | fruit juice | フルーツジュース | Foo-roo-tsoo-jyoo-soo |

bacon
ベーコン
Beh-kohn

banana
バナナ
Bah-nah-nah

berries
ベリー
Beh-ree

biscuit
ビスケット
Bee-soo-keht-to

blueberries
ブルーベリー
Boo-roo-beh-ree

bread
パン
Pahn

jam
ジャム
Jah-moo

butter
バター
Bah-tah

cereal
シリアル
Shee-ree-ah-roo

cheese
チーズ
Chee-zoo

cottage cheese
カッテージチーズ
Kaht-the-jee-chee-zoo

doughnut
ドーナツ
Doh-nah-tsoo

egg
たまご
Tah-mah-goh

ham
ハム
Hah-moo

honey
蜂蜜
Hah-chee-mee-tsoo

marmalade
マーマレード
Mah-mah-reh-doh

omelette
オムレツ
Oh-moo-reh-tsoo

pancake
パンケーキ
Pahn-keh-kee

peanut butter
ピーナッツバター
Pee-nah-tsoo-bah-tah

sandwich
サンドイッチ
Sahn-doh-eet-chee

sausage
ソーセージ
Soh-seh-jee

toast
トースト
Toh-soo-toh

waffle
ワッフル
Wah-foo-roo

yoghurt
ヨーグルト
Yoh-goo-roo-toh

breakfast
朝食
Choh-shoh-koo

brunch
ブランチ
Boo-rahn-chee

porridge
ポリッジ
Poh-reet-jee

scrambled eggs
スクランブルエッグ
Soo-koo-rahn-boo-roo-ehg-goo

hard-boiled egg
茹でたまご
Yoo-deh-tah-mah-goh

soft-boiled egg
半熟たまご
Hahn-jyoo-koo-tah-mah-goh

What do you eat for breakfast?	朝食になにを食べますか。	Choh-shoh-koo nee nah-nee woh tah-beh-mas-kah
When do you have breakfast?	いつ朝食を食べますか	Ee-tsoo choh-shoh-koo woh tah-beh-mas-kah
When does breakfast start?	朝食は何時からですか。	Choh-shoh-koo wah nahn-jee kah-rah des-kah
What would you like to drink?	なにか飲みますか	Nah-nee kah noh-mee-mas-kah
I would like a white tea.	ミルクティーを下さい。	Mee-roo-koo-tee woh koo-dah-sah-ee

bacon
ベーコン
Beh-kohn

beef
牛肉
Gyoo-nee-koo

chicken
鶏肉
Toh-ree-nee-koo

duck
鴨
Kah-moh

ham
ハム
Hah-moo

Kidneys
腎臓
Jeehn-zoh

lamb
ラム肉
Rah-moo-nee-koo

liver
レバー
Reh-bah

mince
ミンチ
Meehn-chee

pâté
パテ
Pah-teh

salami
サラミ
Sah-rah-mee

meat
肉
Nee-koo

rabbit
ウサギ肉
Oo-sah-gee-nee-koo

pork
豚肉
Boo-tah-nee-koo

sausage
ソーセージ
Soh-seh-jee

turkey
七面鳥
Shee-chee-mehn-choh

veal
子牛肉
Koh-oo-shee-nee-koo

fruits
フルーツ
Foo-roo-tsoo

apple
りんご
Reehn-goh

apricot
アプリコット
Ah-poo-ree-koht-toh

banana
バナナ
Bah-nah-nah

blackberry
ブラックベリー
Boo-rahk-koo-beh-ree

blackcurrant
黒すぐり
Koo-roh-soo-goo-ree

blueberry
ブルーベリー
Boo-roo-beh-ree

cherry
さくらんぼ
Sah-koo-rahn-boh

coconut
ココナッツ
Koh-koh-nah-tsoo

fig
いちじく
Ee-chee-jee-koo

grape
ぶどう
Boo-doh

grapefruit
グレープフルーツ
Goo-reh-poo-foo-roo-tsoo

kiwi fruit
キウイ
Kee-wee

lemon
レモン
Reh-mohn

lime
ライム
Rah-ee-moo

mango
マンゴー
Mahn-goh

melon
メロン
Meh-rohn

orange
オレンジ
Oh-rehn-jee

peach
もも
Moh-moh

pear
梨
Nah-shee

pineapple
パイナップル
Pah-eehn-ahp-poo-roo

lychee
ライチ
Rah-ee-chee

clementine
みかん
Mee-kahn

papaya
パパイア
Pah-pah-ee-ah

kumqvat
金柑
Keehn-kahn

raspberry
ラズベリー
Rah-zoo-beh-ree

plum
プラム
Poo-rah-moo

watermelon
すいか
Soo-ee-kah

nectarine
ネクタリン
Neh-koo-tah-reehn

persimmon
柿
Kah-kee

redcurrant
すぐり
Soo-goo-ree

rhubarb
ルバーブ
Roo-bah-boo

pomegranate
ザクロ
Zah-koo-roh

strawberry
いちご
Ee-chee-goh

passion fruit
パッションフルーツ
Pahs-shohn-foo-roo-tsoo

vegetables
野菜
Yah-sah-ee

artichoke
アーティチョーク
Ah-tee-choh-koo

asparagus
アスパラガス
Ah-soo-pah-rah-gah-soo

avocado
アボカド
Ah-boh-kah-doh

beansprouts
もやし
Moh-yah-shee

beetroot
ビーツ
Bee-tsoo

broccoli
ブロッコリー
Boo-rohk-koh-ree

Brussels sprouts
芽キャベツ
Meh-kya-beh-tsoo

cabbage
キャベツ
Kyah-beh-tsoo

aubergine
なす
Nah-soo

carrot
にんじん
Neehn-jeehn

cauliflower
カリフラワー
Kah-re-foo-rah-wah

celery
セロリ
Seh-roh-ree

courgette
ズッキーニ
Zook-kee-nee

cucumber
きゅうり
Kyoo-ree

garlic
にんにく
Nihn-nee-koo

ginger
しょうが
Shoh-gah

leek
ねぎ
Neh-gee

lettuce
レタス
Reh-tah-soo

mushroom
マッシュルーム
Mahs-shoo-roo-moo

onion
玉ねぎ
Tah-mah-neh-gee

peas
さやえんどう
Dah-yah-ehn-doh

potato
じゃがいも
Jyah-gah-ee-moh

pumpkin
カボチャ
Kah-boh-chah

spinach
ほうれん草
Hoh-rehn-soh

radish
ラディッシュ
Rah-dee-shoo

sweetcorn
スイートコーン
Soo-ee-toh-kohn

tomato
トマト
Toh-mah-toh

spring onion
青ネギ
Ah-oh-neh-gee

red pepper
レッドペッパー
Reht-toh-pehp-pah

green beans
グリーンピース
Goo-reehn-pee-soo

chicory
チコリー
Chee-koh-ree

turnip
カブ
Kah-boo

cuttlefish
コウイカ
Koh-ee-kah

haddock
コダラ
Koh-dah-rah

lemon sole
カレイ
Kah-reh-ee

halibut
オヒョウ
Oh-hyoh

mackerel
さば
Sah-bah

monkfish
アンコウ
Ahn-koh

mussels
ムール貝
Moo-roo-gah-ee

sardine
イワシ
Ee-wah-shee

sea bass
シーバス
Shee-bah-soo

sea bream
タイ
Tah-ee

swordfish
メカジキ
Meh-kah-jee-ke

trout
マス
Mah-soo

crab
カニ
Kah-nee

crayfish
ザリガニ
Zah-ree-gah-nee

lobster
ロブスター
Roh-boo-soo-tah

tuna
マグロ
Mah-goo-roh

octopus
タコ
Tah-koh

oyster
牡蠣
Kah-kee

prawn / shrimp
エビ
Eh-bee

scallop
ホタテ
Hoh-tah-teh

salmon
サケ
Sah-keh

squid
イカ
Ee-kah

fish	魚	Sah-kah-nah
cleaned	清潔	Seh-ee-keh-tsoo
fresh	新鮮	Sheen-sehn
frozen	冷凍	Reh-ee-toh
salted	塩漬けの	Shee-oh-tsoo-keh
skinned	皮を剥いだ	Kah-wah woh-hah-ee-dah
smoked	燻製	Koon-seh-ee

milk
牛乳
Gyoo-nyoo

cottage cheese
カッテージチーズ
Kaht-the-jee-chee-zoo

cheese
チーズ
Chee-zoo

cream
クリーム
Koo-ree-moo

blue cheese
ブルーチーズ
Boo-roo-chee-zoo

egg
たまご
Tah-mah-goh

butter
バター
Bah-tah

goat's cheese	ヤギチーズ	Yah-gee-chee-zoo
margarine	マーガリン	Mah-gah-reen
full-fat milk	全脂肪ミルク	Zehn-shee-boh-mee-roo-koo
semi-skimmed milk	クリームの一部が取除かれたミルク	Koo-ree-moo noh ee-chee-boo gah Noh-zoh-kah-reh-tah mee-roo-koo

skimmed milk	スキムミルク	Soo-kee-moo-mee-roo-koo
sour cream	サワークリーム	Saah-wah-koo-ree-moo
yoghurt	ヨーグルト	Yoh-goo-roo-toh
crème fraîche	生クリーム	Nah-mah-koo-ree-moo

baguette
バゲット
Ba-geht-toh

bread rolls
パン
Pahn

brown bread
黒パン
Koo-roh-pahn

cake
ケーキ
Keh-kee

loaf
食パン
Shoh-koo-pahn

white bread
白いパン
Shee-roh-ee-pahn

garlic bread	ガーリックトースト	Gah-reek-koo-toh-soo-toh	quiche	キッシュ	Kees-shoo
pastry	ペストリー	Peh-soo-toh-ree	sliced loaf	食パン	Shoh-koo-pahn
pitta bread	ピタパン	Pee-tah-pahn	sponge cake	スポンジケーキ	Soo-pohn-gee-keh-kee

ketchup
ケチャップ
Keh-chahp-poo

mayonnaise
マヨネーズ
Mah-yoh-neh-zoo

mustard
マスタード
Mah-soo-tah-doh

vinegar
酢
Soo

salt
しお
Shee-oh

pepper
こしょう
Koh-shoh

basil	バジル	Bah-jee-roo	paprika	パプリカ	Pah-poo-ree-kah
chilli powder	唐辛子	Toh-gah-rah-shee	parsley	パセリ	Pah-seh-ree
chives	チャイブ	Chah-ee-boo	rosemary	ローズマリー	Roh-soo-mah-ree
cinnamon	シナモン	Shee-nah-mohn	saffron	サフラン	Sah-foo-rahn
coriander	コリアンダー	Koh-ree-ahn-dah	sage	サージ	Sah-jee
cumin	クミン	Koo-meehn	salad dressing	サラダドレッシング	Sah-rah-dah-doh-reh-sheehn-goo
curry	カレー粉	Kah-reh-koh	spices	スパイス	Soo-pah-ee-soo
dill	ディル	Dee-roo	thyme	タイム	Tah-ee-moo
nutmeg	ナツメグ	Nah-tsoo-meh-goo	vinaigrette	ヴィネグッレットソース	Bee-neh-goo-reht-toh-soh-soo

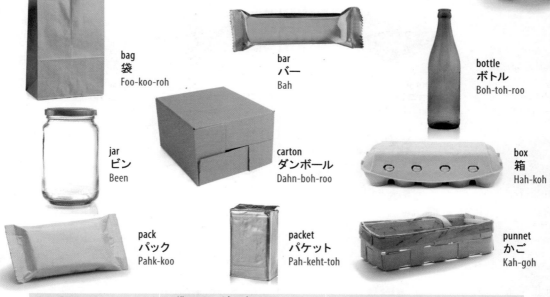

bag
袋
Foo-koo-roh

bar
バー
Bah

bottle
ボトル
Boh-toh-roo

jar
ビン
Been

carton
ダンボール
Dahn-boh-roo

box
箱
Hah-koh

pack
パック
Pahk-koo

packet
パケット
Pah-keht-toh

punnet
かご
Kah-goh

a bag of potatoes	一袋のじゃがいも	Hee-toh-boo-koo-roh noh jyah-gah-ee-moh
chocolate bar	チョコバー	Choh-koh-bah
two bottles of mineral water	二本のミネラルウォーター	Nee-hohn noh mee-neh-rah-roo-woh-tah
a carton of milk	牛乳パックを一つ	Gyoo-nyoo-pahk-koo woh hee-toh-tsoo
a jar of jam	ジャムのビンを一つ	Jya-moo been woh hee-toh-tsoo

biscuit
ビスケット
Bee-soo-keht-toh

chocolate
チョコレート
Choh-koh-reh-toh

chocolate cake
チョコレートケーキ
Choh-koh-reh-toh-keh-kee

apple pie
アップルパイ
Ahp-poo-roo-pah-ee

doughnut
ドーナツ
Doh-nah-tsoo

fruit cake
フルーツケーキ
Foo-roo-tsoo-keh-kee

fruit salad
フルーツサラダ
Foo-roo-tsoo-sah-rah-dah

cheesecake
チーズケーキ
Chee-zoo-keh-kee

gingerbread
ジンジャーブレット
Jeehn-jah-boo-reht-toh

ice cream
アイスクリーム
Ah-ee-soo-koo-ree-moo

muffin
マフィン
Mah-feen

chocolate mousse
チョコレートムース
Choh-koh-reh-toh Moo-soo

milkshake
ミルクシェーク
Mee-roo-koo-sheh-koo

marshmallow
マシュマロ
Mah-shoo-mah-roh

macaroon
マカロン
Mah-kah-rohn

waffle
ワッフル
Wah-foo-roo

pancakes
パンケーキ
Pahn-keh-kee

strudel
シュトゥルーデル
Shoo-too-roo-deh-roo

pudding
プリン
Poo-reen

honey
蜂蜜
Ha-chee-mee-tsoo

cake	ケーキ	Keh-kee
coconut cake	ココナッツケーキ	Koh-koh-nah-tsoo keh-kee
dessert	デザート	Deh-zah-toh
frozen yoghurt	フローズンヨーグルト	Foo-roh-zoon-yoh-goo-roo-toh
rice pudding	ライスプディング	Rah-ee-soo-poo-deen-goo
I like to eat sweets.	甘いものが好き	Ah-mah-ee moh-noh gah soo-kee
I cannot eat anything sweet.	甘いものが食べれない	Ah-mah-ee moh-noh gah tah-beh-reh-nah-ee

cheeseburger
チーズバーガー
Chee-zoo-bah-gah

hot dog
ホットドッグ
Hoht-toh-dohg-goo

fish sandwich
フィッシュサンドイッチ
Feesh-shoo-sahn-doh-eet-chee

fried chicken
フライドチキン
Foo-rah-ee-doh-chee-kehn

French fries
フライドポテト
Foo-rah-ee-doh-poh-the-toh

nachos
ナチョス
Nah-cho-soo

taco
タコス
Tah-koh-soo

burrito
ブリトー
Boo-ree-toh

pizza
ピザ
Pee-zah

hamburger
ハンバーガー
Hahn-bah-gah

chicken sandwich
チキンサンドイッチ
Chee-kehn-sahn-doh-eet-chee

fish and chips
フィッシュアンドチップス
Feesh-shoo-ahn-doh-cheep-poo-soo

to peel	皮を剥く	Kah-wah woh moo-koo
to grate	すりおろす	Soo-ree-oh-roh-soo
to chop	きざむ	Kee-zah-moo
to crush	つぶす	Tsoo-boo-soo
to beat	叩く	Tah-tah-koo
to grease	油を引く	Ah-boo-rah woh hee-koo
to break	折る	Oh-roo
to stir	かき混ぜる	Mah-kee-mah-zeh-roo
to knead	こねる	Koh-neh-roo
to steam	蒸す	Moo-soo
to weigh	量る	Hah-kah-roo
to add	加える	Koo-wah-eh-roo
to bake	焼く	Yah-koo
to stir-fry	炒める	EE-tah-meh-roo
to grill	焼く	Yah-koo
to roast	ローストする	Roh-soo-toh-soo-roo
to barbecue	バーベキューする	Bah-beh-kyoo-soo-roo
to fry	揚げる	Ah-geh-roo

to wash
洗う
Ah-rah-oo

to cut
切る
Kee-roo

to mix
混ぜる
Mah-zeh-roo

to boil
茹でる
Yoo-deh-roo

bar
バー
Bah-ah

buffet
ビュッフェ
Byuf-feh

bill
会計
Kah-ee-keh-ee

bistro
ビストロ
Bee-soo-toh-roh

café
カフェ
Ka-feh

dessert
デザート
Deh-zah-toh

menu
メニュー
Meh-nyoo

canteen
食堂
Shoh-koo-doh

pizzeria
ピザ屋
Pee-zah-yah

pub
パブ
Pah-boo

salad bar
サラダバー
Sah-rah-dah-bah

deli
総菜屋
Soh-za-ee-yah

self-service
セルフサービス
Seh-roo-foo-sah-bee-soo

take-out / take-away
持ち帰り
Moh-chee-kah-eh-ree

waiter
ウェイター
Oo-eh-ee-tah

waitress
ウェイトレス
Oo-eh-ee-toh-reh-soo

à la carte	アラカルト	Ah-rah-kah-roo-toh
starter	前菜	Zehn-sa-ee
booking	予約	Yoh-yah-koo
complimentary	無料	Moo-ryo
dish	皿	Sah-rah
main course	メインコース	Meh-een-koh-soo
to order	注文する	Choo-mohn soo-roo
speciality	名物	Meh-ee-boo-tsoo
aperitif	食前酒	Shoh-koo-sehn-shoo

What do you want to order?	なにを注文する?	Nah-nee woh choo-mohn soo-roo?
I would like to see the menu.	メニューをみたいのですが。	Meh-nyoo woh mee-tah-ee noh des-gah
We'll take the set menu.	セットメニューを頼みます。	Seht-toh meh-nyoo woh tah-noh-mee-mah-soo

TRAVEL AND LEISURE

to travel by bus
バス旅行
Bah-soo-ryo-koh

to travel by plane
飛行機で旅行する
Hee-koh-kee deh ryo-koh soo-roo

to travel by car
車で旅行する
Koo-roo-mah deh ryo-koh soo-roo

to travel by bicycle
自転車旅行
Jee-tehn-shah ryo-koh

to travel by motorcycle
バイク旅行
Bah-ee-koo ryo-koh

travel agency
旅行代理店
Ruo-koh-dah-ee-ree-tehn

family holiday
家族休暇
Kah-zoh-koo Kyoo-kah

safari
サファリ
Sah-fah-ree

honeymoon
ハネムーン
Hah-neh-moon

beach holiday
ビーチで休暇
Bee-chee deh kyoo-kah

round-the-world trip
世界一周旅行
Seh-kah-ee ee-shoo ryo-koh

cruise
クルーズ
Koo-roo-zoo

to book
予約
Yoh-yah-koo

long-haul destination
長距離目的地
Choh-kyo-ree moh-koo-teh-kee-chee

guided tour
ガイドツアー
Gah-ee-doh tsoo-ah

out of season
オフシーズン
Oh-foo-shee-zoon

picturesque village
絵のように美しい村
Eh noh-yoh-nee oo-tsoo-koo-shee moo-rah

landscape
景色
Keh-shee-kii

to go sightseeing
観光に行く
Kahn-koh nee ee-koo

city break
街で休暇
Mah-chee deh kyoo-kah

holiday brochure	パフレット	Pahn-foo-reht-toh
holiday destination	旅行先	Ryo-koh sah-kee
package tour	パッケージツアー	Pahk-keh-jee tsoo-ah
places of interest	興味のある場所	Kyo-mee noh ah-roo bah-shoh
short break	小休憩	Koh-kyoo-ke-ee
tourist attractions	観光スポット	Kahn-koh soo-poht-toh
tourist trap	ぼったくり	Boht-tah-koo-ree

Afghanistan
アフガニスタン
Ah-foo-gah-nee-soo-tahn

Angola
アンゴラ
Ahn-goh-rah

Aruba
アルバ
Ah-roo-bah

The Bahamas
バハマ
Bah-hah-mah

Belarus
ベラルーシ
Beh-rah-roo-shee

Albania
アルバニア
Ah-roo-bah-nee-ah

Antigua and Barbuda
アンティグア・バーブ
ーダ
Ahn-tee-goo-ah bah-boo-dah

Australia
オーストラリア
Oh-soo-toh-rah-ree-ah

Bahrain
バーレーン
Bah-rehn

Belgium
ベルギー
Beh-roo-gee

Algeria
アルジェリア
Ah-roo-jeh-ree-ah

Argentina
アルゼンチン
Ah-roo-zehn-teen

Austria
オーストリア
Oh-soo-toh-ree-ah

Bangladesh
バングラディッシュ
Bahn-goo-rah-desh-shoo

Belize
ベリーズ
Beh-ree-soo

Andorra
アンドラ
Ahn-doh-rah

Armenia
アルメニア
Ah-roo-meh-nee-ah

Azerbaijan
アゼルバイジャン
Ah-zeh-roo-bah-ee-jyahn

Barbados
バルバドス
Bah-roo-bah-doh-soo

Benin
ベナン
Beh-nahn

Bhutan
ブータン
Boo-tahn

Brazil
ブラジル
Boo-rah-jee-roo

Burma
ブルマ
Boo-roo-mah

Canada
カナダ
Kah-nah-dah

Chile
チリ
Chee-ree

Bolivia
ボリビア
Bo-ree-bee-ah

Brunei
ブルネイ
Boo-roo-neh-ee

Burundi
ブルンジ
Boo-roon-jee

Cape Verde
カーボベルデ
Kah-boh beh-roo-deh

China
中国
Choo-goh-koo

Bosnia and Herzegovina
ボスニア・ヘルツェ
ゴビナ
Boh-soo-nee-ah heh-roo-
tseh-goh-bee-nah

Bulgaria
ブルガリア
Boo-roo-gah-ree-ah

Cambodia
カンボジア
Kahn-boh-jee-ah

Central African Republic
中央アフリカ共和国
Choo-oh ah-foo-ree-kah kyoh-wah-
koh-koo

Colombia
コロンビア
Koh-rohn-bee-ah

Botswana
ボツワナ
Boh-tsoo-wah-nah

Burkina Faso
ブルキナファソ
Boo-roo-kee-nah-fah-soh

Cameroon
カメルーン
Kah-meh-roon

Chad
チャド
Chah-doh

Comoros
コモロ
Koh-moh-roh

**Democratic Republic
of the Congo
コンゴ民主共和国**
Kohn-goh meen-shoo-
kyoh-wah-koh-koo

**Côte d'Ivoire
コートジボワール**
Koh-toh-jee-boh-wah-roo

**Cyprus
キプロス**
Kee-poo-roh-soo

**Dominica
ドミニカ**
Doh-mee-nee-kah

**Egypt
エジプト**
Eh-jee-poo-toh

**Croatia
クロアチア**
Koo-roh-ah-chee-ah

**Czechia
チェコ**
Cheh-koh

**Dominican Republic
ドミニカ共和国**
Doh-mee-nee-kah-kyoh-wah-
koh-koo

**El Salvador
エルサルバドル**
Eh-roo-sah-roo-bah-doh-roo

**Republic of the Congo
コンゴ共和国**
Kohn-goh kyoh-wah-
koh-koo

**Cuba
キューバ**
Kyoo-bah

**Denmark
デンマーク**
Dehn-mah-koo

**East Timor
東ティモール**
Hee-gah-shee-tee-moh-roo

**Equatorial Guinea
赤道ギニア**
Seh-kee-doh-gee-neh-ah

**Costa Rica
コスタリカ**
Koh-soo-tah-ree-kah

**Curacao
キュラソー島**
Kyoo-rah-soh-toh

**Djibouti
ジブチ**
Jee-boo-chee

**Ecuador
エクアドル**
Eh-koo-ah-doh-roo

**Eritrea
エリトリア**
Eh-ree-toh-ree-ah

Estonia
エストニア
Eh-soo-toh-nee-ah

France
フランス
Foo-rahn-soo

Germany
ドイツ
Doh-ee-tsoo

Guatemala
グアテマラ
Goo-ah-teh-mah-rah

Haiti
ハイチ
Hah-ee-chee

Ethiopia
エチオピア
Eh-chee-oh-pee-ah

Gabon
ガボン
Gah-bohn

Ghana
ガーナ
Gah-nah

Guinea
ギニア
Gee-nee-ah

Honduras
ホンジュラス
Hohn-jyoo-rah-soo

Fiji
フィジー
Fee-jee

The Gambia
ガンビア
Gahn-bee-ah

Greece
ギリシャ
Gee-ree-shah

Guinea-Bissau
ギニアビサウ
Gee-nee-ah bee-sah-oo

Hong Kong
香港
Hohn-kohn

Finland
フィンランド
Feen-rahn-doh

Georgia
グルジア
Goo-roo-jee-ah

Grenada
グラナダ
Goo-rah-nah-dah

Guyana
ガイアナ
Gah-ee-ah-nah

Hungary
ハンガリー
Hahn-gah-ree

Iceland
アイスランド
Ah-ee-soo-rahn-doh

Iraq
イラク
Ee-rah-koo

Jamaica
ジャマイカ
Jyah-mah-ee-kah

Kenya
ケニア
Keh-nee-ah

Kosovo
コソボ
Koh-soh-boh

India
インド
Een-doh

Ireland
アイルランド
Ah-ee-roo-rahn-doh

Japan
日本
Nee-hohn

Kiribati
キリバス
Kee-ree-bah-soo

Kuwait
クウェート
Koo-weh-toh

Indonesia
インドネシア
Een-doh-neh-shee-ah

Israel
イスラエル
Ee-soo-rah-eh-roo

Jordan
ヨルダン
Yoh-roo-dahn

North Korea
北朝鮮
Kee-tah-choh-sehn

Kyrgyzstan
キルギス
Kee-roo-gee-soo

Iran
イラン
Ee-rahn

Italy
イタリア
Ee-tah-ree-ah

Kazakhstan
カザフスタン
Kah-za-foo-soo-tahn

South Korea
韓国
Kahn-koh-koo

Laos
ラオス
Rah-oh-soo

Latvia
ラトビア
Rah-toh-bee-ah

Libya
リビア
Ree-bee-ah

Macau
マカオ
Mah-kah-oh

Malaysia
マレーシア
Mah-reh-shee-ah

Marshall Islands
マーシャル諸島
Mah-shah-roo
shoh-toh

Lebanon
レバノン
Reh-bah-nohn

Liechtenstein
リヒテンシュタイン
Ree-hee-tehn-shoo-tah-een

Macedonia
マケドニア
Mah-seh-doh-nee-ah

Maldives
モルディブ
Moh-roo-dee-boo

Mauritania
モーリタニア
Moh-ree-tah-nee-ah

Lesotho
レソト
Reh-soh-toh

Lithuania
リトアニア
Ree-toh-ah-nee-ah

Madagascar
マダガスカル
Mah-dah-gah-soo-kah-roo

Mali
マリ
Mah-ree

Mauritius
モーリシャス
Moh-ree-shah-soo

Liberia
リベリア
Ree-beh-ree-ah

Luxembourg
ルクセンブルク
Roo-koo-sehn-boo-roo-goo

Malawi
マラウイ
Mah-rah-oo-ee

Malta
マルタ
Mah-roo-tah

Mexico
メキシコ
Meh-kee-shee-koh

Micronesia
ミクロネシア
Mee-koo-roh-neh-shee-ah

Montenegro
モンテネグロ
Mohn-teh-neh-goo-roh

Nauru
ナウル
Nah-oo-roo

Nicaragua
ニカラグア
Nee-kah-rah-goo-ah

Oman
オマーン
Oh-mahn

Moldova
モルドバ
Moh-roo-doh-bah

Morocco
モロッコ
Moh-rohk-koh

Nepal
ネパール
Neh-pah-roo

Niger
ニジェール
Nee-jeh-roo

Pakistan
パキスタン
Pah-kee-soo-tahn

Monaco
モナコ
Moh-nah-koh

Mozambique
モザンビーク
Moh-zahn-bee-koo

Netherlands
オランダ
Oh-rahn-dah

Nigeria
ナイジェリア
Nah-ee-jeh-ree-ah

Palau
パラオ
Pah-rah-oh

Mongolia
モンゴル
Mohn-goh-roo

Namibia
ナミビア
Nahn-bee-ah

New Zealand
ニュージーランド
Nyoo-jee-rahn-doh

Norway
ノルウェー
Noh-roo-eh

Palestinian Territories
パレスチナ自治区
Pah-reh-soo-chee-nah
Jee-chee-koo

Panama
パナマ
Pah-nah-mah

Papua New Guinea
パプアニューギニア
Pah-poo-ah nyoo-gee-nee-ah

Paraguay
パラグアイ
Pah-rah-goo-ah-ee

Peru
ペルー
Peh-roo

Philippines
フィリピン
Fee-ree-peehn

Poland
ポーランド
Poh-rahn-doh

Portugal
ポルトガル
Poh-roo-toh-gah-roo

Qatar
カタール
Kah-tah-roo

Romania
ルーマニア
Roo-mah-nee-ah

Russia
ロシア
Roh-shee-ah

Rwanda
ルワンダ
Roo-wahn-dah

Saint Lucia
セントルシア
Sehn-toh-roo-shee-ah

Samoa
サモア
Sah-moh-ah

San Marino
サンマリノ
Sahn-mah-ree-noh

Saudi Arabia
サウジアラビア
Sah-oo-jee-ah-rah-bee-ah

Senegal
セネガル
Seh-neh-gah-roo

Serbia
セルビア
Seh-roo-bee-ah

Seychelles
セーシェル
Seh-shee-roo

Sierra Leone
シエラレオネ
Shee-eh-rah-reh-oh-neh

127

Singapore
シンガポール
Sheen-gah-poh-roo

Solomon Islands
ソロモン諸島
Soh-roh-mohn-shoh-toh

Sri Lanka
スリランカ
Soo-ree-rahn-kah

Swaziland
スワジランド
Soo-wah-jee-rahn-doh

Taiwan
台湾
Tah-ee-wahn

Sint Maarten
サンマルタン島
Sahn-mah-roo-than-toh

Somalia
ソマリア
Soh-mah-ree-ah

Sudan
スーダン
Soo-dahn

Sweden
スウェーデン
Soo-weh-dehn

Tajikistan
タジキスタン
Tah-jee-kee-soo-tahn

Slovakia
スロバキア
Soo-roh-bah-kee-ah

South Africa
南アフリカ
Mee-nah-mee-ah-foo-ree-kah

South Sudan
南スーダン
Mee-nah-mee-soo-dahn

Switzerland
スイス
Soo-ee-soo

Tanzania
タンザニア
Than-zah-nee-ah

Slovenia
スロベニア
Soo-roh-beh-nee-ah

Spain
スペイン
Soo-peh-een

Suriname
スリナム
Soo-ree-nah-moo

Syria
シリア
Shee-ree-ah

Thailand
タイ
Tah-ee

Togo
トーゴ
Toh-goh

Turkey
トルコ
Toh-roo-koh

Ukraine
ウクライナ
Oo-koo-rah-ee-nah

Uruguay
ウルグアイ
Oo-roo-goo-ah-ee

Vietnam
ベトナム
Beh-toh-nah-moo

Tonga
トンガ
Tohn-gah

Turkmenistan
トルクメニスタン
Toh-roo-koo-meh-nees-tahn

United Arab Emirates
アラブ首長国連邦
Ah-rah-boo-shoo-choh-
koh-koo-rehn-poh

Uzbekistan
ウズベキスタン
Oo-zoo-beh-kees-tahn

Yemen
イエメン
Ee-eh-mehn

Trinidad and Tobago
トリニダード・トバゴ
Toh-ree-nee-dah-doh-toh-
bah-goh

Tuvalu
ツバル
Tsoo-bah-roo

United Kingdom
イギリス
Ee-gee-ree-soo

Vanuatu
バヌアツ
Bah-noo-ah-tsoo

Zambia
ザンビア
Zahn-bee-ah

Tunisia
チュニジア
Choo-nee-shee-ah

Uganda
ウガンダ
Oo-gahn-dah

United States of America
アメリカ
Ah-meh-ree-kah

Venezuela
ベネズエラ
Beh-neh-zoo-eh-rah

Zimbabwe
ジンバブエ
Jeehn-bah-boo-eh

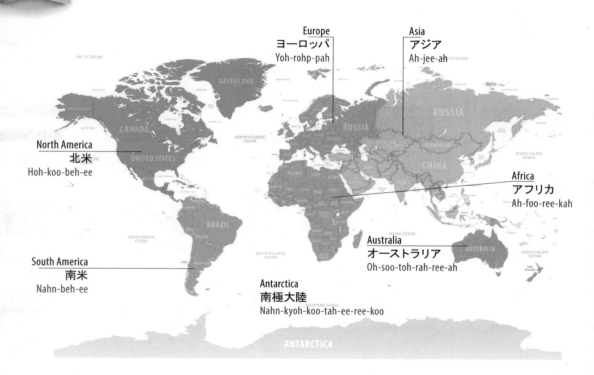

Europe
ヨーロッパ
Yoh-rohp-pah

Asia
アジア
Ah-jee-ah

North America
北米
Hoh-koo-beh-ee

Africa
アフリカ
Ah-foo-ree-kah

South America
南米
Nahn-beh-ee

Australia
オーストラリア
Oh-soo-toh-rah-ree-ah

Antarctica
南極大陸
Nahn-kyoh-koo-tah-ee-ree-koo

bus stop
バス停
Bah-soo-teh-ee

platform
プラットフォーム
Poo-raht-toh-foh-moo

(aero)plane
飛行機
Hee-koh-kee

moped / scooter
スクーター
Soo-koo-tah

(bi)cycle
自転車
Jee-tehn-shah

boat
ボート
Boh-toh

bus
バス
Bah-soo

ship
船
Foo-neh

car
車
Koo-roo-mah

helicopter
ヘリコプター
Heh-ree-kohp-poo-tah

lorry
トラック
Toh-rahk-koo

tanker
タンカー
Than-kah

kid's scooter
キッズスケーター
Keed-zoo soo-keh-tah

(motor)bike
バイク
Ba-ee-koo

train
列車
Rehs-shah

taxi
タクシー
Tah-koo-shee

ferry
フェリー
Feh-ree

submarine
潜水艦
Sehn-soo-ee-kahn

sailing boat
セーリングボート
Seh-reen-goo boh-toh

tram
路面電車
Roh-mehn-dehn-shah

by air	飛行機で	Hee-koh-kee deh	in the port	港に	Mee-nah-toh nee
on the motorway	高速道路で	Koh-soh-koo-doh-roh deh	by rail	列車で	Rehs-shah deh
on the road	路上で	Roh-jyoh deh	by tube / underground	地下鉄で	Chee-kah-teh-tsoo deh
by sea	海で	Oo-mee deh	on foot	徒歩で	Toh-hoh deh

airport
空港
Koo-koh

arrivals
到着
Toh-chah-koo

departures
出発
Shoop-pah-tsoo

luggage
荷物
nee-moh-tsoo

carry-on luggage
手荷物
Teh-nee-moh-tsoo

oversized baggage
大きすぎる荷物
Oh-kee-soo-gee-roo nee-moh-tsoo

check-in desk
チェックインカウンター
Chehk-koo-een kah-oon-tah

customs
税関
Zeh-kahn

baggage reclaim
荷物受取所
nee-moh-tsoo oo-keh-toh-ree-shoh

boarding pass
搭乗券
Toh-jyoh-kehn

flight ticket
航空券
Koh-koo-kehn

economy class
エコノミークラス
Eh-koh-noh-mee koo-rah-soo

business class
ビジネスクラス
Bee-jee-neh-soo koo-rah-soo

arrivals lounge
到着ラウンジ
Toh-chah-koo rah-oon-jee

delayed
遅延
Chee-ehn

to board a plane
飛行機に乗る
Hee-koh-kee nee noh-roo

gate
ゲート
Geh-toh

passport
パスポート
Pah-soo-poh-toh

passport control
入国審査
Nyoo-koh-koo-sheen-sah

security check
セキュリティーチェック
Seh-kyoo-ree-tee-chehk-koo

airline	航空会社	Koh-koo-gah-ee-shah
boarding time	搭乗時間	Toh-jyo-jee-kahn
charter flight	チャーター便	Chah-tah-been
on time	定刻	Teh-ee-koh-koo
one-way ticket	片道切符	Kah-tah-mee-chee-keep-poo
return ticket	帰りの切符	Kah-eh-ree noh keep-poo

long-haul flight	長距離飛行	Choh-kyoh-ree-hee-koh
The flight has been delayed.	フライトが遅れました。	Foo-rah-ee-toh ah oh-koo-reh-mah-shee-tah.
to book a ticket to...	チケットを予約する。	Chee-keht-toh woh yoh-yah-koo soo-roo

railway station
駅
Eh-kee

train
列車
Rehs-shah

platform
プラットフォーム
Poo-raht-toh-foh-moo

express train	特急列車	Toht-kyoo-rehs-shah
to get on the train	列車に乗る	Rehs-shah nee noh-roo
to get off the train	列車を降りる	Rehs-shah woh oh-ree-roo
to miss a train	列車に乗り遅れる	Rehs-shah nee noh-ree oh-koo-reh-roo

train driver
列車の運転手
Rehs-shah noh oon-tehn-shoo

travelcard
乗車券
Jyoh-shah-kehn

train journey
列車旅
Rehs-sha tah-bee

carriage
車両
Shah-ryoh

seat
席
Seh-kee

station
駅
Eh-kee

restaurant car
食堂車
Shoh-koo-doh-shah

sleeper train
寝台列車
Sheen-dah-ee rehs-shah

toilet
トイレ
Toh-ee-reh

coach
長距離バス
Choh-kyo-ree bah-soo

bus driver
バス運転手
Bah-soo oon-tehn-shoo

bus stop
バス停
Bah-soo teh-ee

validator
バリデータ
Bah-ree-deh-tah

double-decker bus
２階建てバス
Nee-kah-ee-dah-teh-bah-soo

bus journey
バスの旅
Bah-soo noh tah-be

coach station
バスターミナル
Bah-soo tah-mee-nah-roo

request stop
リクエストバス停
Ree-koo-eh-soo-toh bah-soo-teh-ee

bus fare	バス賃	Bah-soo cheen
the next stop	次の駅	Tsoo-gee noh eh-kee
night bus	夜行バス	Yah-koh bah-soo
to get on the bus	バスに乗る	Bah-soo nee noh-roo
to get off the bus	バスを降りる	Bah-soo woh oh-ree-roo
to miss a bus	バスに乗り遅れる	Bah-soo nee noh-ree-oh-koo-reh-roo

hotel
ホテル
Hoh-teh-roo

campsite
キャンプ場
Kyan-poo-jyoh

holiday resort
行楽地
Koh-rah-koo-chee

youth hostel
ユースホステル
Yoo-soo hoh-soo-teh-roo

accommodation	宿泊設備	Shoo-koo-hah-koo seh-tsoo-bee
all-inclusive	全て込みの	Soo-beh-teh-koh-mee-noh
half-board	二食付き	Nee-shoh-koo-tsoo-kee
full-board	三食付き	Sahn-shoh-koo-tsoo-kee
self-catering	自炊	Jee-soo-ee
Can you recommend a hotel?	オススメのホテルはありますか?	Oh-soo-soo-meh noh hoh-teh-roo wah ah-ree-mas-kah?
We are staying at the hotel "XZ".	私達はXZホテルに泊まってます。	Wah-tah-shee wah XZ hoh-teh-roo nee toh-maht-teh mas
Have you already booked the hotel?	すでにホテルは予約しましたか?	Soo-deh nee hoh-teh-roo wah yoh-tah-koo shee-mash-tah-kah
I'm looking for a place to stay.	私は滞在する場所を探してます。	Wah-tah-shee wah tah-ee-za-ee soo-roo bah-shoh woh sah-gah-shee-teh-mas

bed and breakfast
朝食付き民宿
Choh-shoh-koo-tsoo-kee meen-shoo-koo

single bed
シングルベッド
Sheen-goo-roo beht-toh

double bed
ダブルベッド
Dah-boo-roo-beht-toh

floor
フロア
Foo-roh-ah

front desk / reception
フロントデスク
Foo-rohn-toh-deh-soo-koo

hotel manager
支配人
Shee-hah-ee-neen

indoor pool
屋内プール
Shee-tsoo-nah-ee-poo-roo

key
カギ
Kah-gee

kitchenette
簡易台所
Kahn-ee dah-ee-doh-koh-roh

luggage cart
荷物カート
Nee-moh-tsoo kah-toh

towels
タオル
Tah-oh-roo

room service
ルームサービス
Roo-moo sah-bee-soo

lobby
ロビー
Roh-bee

wake-up call
モーニングコール
Moh-neen-goo koh-roo

reservation
予約
Yoh-yah-koo

guest
ゲスト
Geh-soo-toh

check-in	チェックイン	Chehk-koo-een
check-out	チェックアウト	Chehk-koo ah-oo-toh
complimentary breakfast	無料の朝食	Moo-ryo noh choh-shoh-koo
king-size bed	キングサイズベッド	Keen-goo sah-ee-zoo-beht-toh
late charge	延滞料金	Ehn-kee ryoh-keen
full	満室	Mahn-shee-tsoo
parking pass	駐車券	Choo-shah-kehn
pay-per-view movie	有料放送映画	Yoo-ryoh hoh-soh-eh-ee-gah
queen-size bed	クイーンサイズベッド	Koo-een-sah-ee-zoo-beht-toh
rate	料金	Ryoh-keen
vacancy	空室	Koo-shee-tsoo

city-centre / downtown
繁華街
Hahn-kah-gah-ee

capital
首都
Shoo-toh

centre
中央
Choo-oh

district
地区
Chee-koo

industrial zone
工業地帯
Koh-gyoh-chee-tah-ee

city
街
Mah-chee

metropolis
大都市
Dah-ee-toh-shee

region
地域
Chee-kee

seaside resort
シーサイドリゾート
Shee-sah-ee-doh ree-zoh-toh

141

old town
旧市街
Kyoo-shee-gah-ee

ski resort
スキー場
Soo-kee jyoh

small town
小さな町
Chee-sah-nah mah-chee

suburb
郊外
Koh-gah-ee

village
村
Moo-rah

winter resort
ウィンターリゾート
Ween-tah ree-zoh-toh

alley
路地
Roh-jee

boulevard
大通り
Oh-doh-ree

motorway
高速道路
Koh-soh-koo doh-roh

country road
田舎道
Ee-nah-kah mee-chee

toll road
有料道路
Yoo-ryo-doh-roh

street
通り
Doh-ree

bicycle lane
自転車レーン
Jee-tehn-shah-rehn

bicycle path
自転車専用道路
Jee-tehn-sha-sehn-yoh-doh-roh

crossroads / intersection
交差点
Koh-sah-tehn

traffic lights
交通信号
Koh-tsoo-sheen-goh

red light
赤信号
Ah-kah-sheen-goh

orange light
黄色信号
Kee-roh-sheen-goh

green light
青信号
Ah-oh-sheen-goh

roundabout
回り道
Mah-wah-ree mee-chee

pedestrian crossing
横断歩道
Oh-dahn-hoh-doh

pavement
歩道
Hoh-doh

bridge
橋
Hah-shee

footbridge
歩道橋
Hoh-doh-bah-shee

overpass
歩道橋
Hoh-doh-bah-shee

underpass
地下道
Chee-kah-doh

tunnel
トンネル
Tohn-neh-roo

road
道
Mee-chee

street corner
街角
Mah-chee-kah-doh

one-way street
一方通行
Eep-poh-tsoo-koh

avenue	通り	Doh-ree
main road	主要道路	Shoo-doh doh-roh
side street	裏通り	Oo-rah-doh-ree
expressway	高速道路	Koh-soh-koo doh-roh
four-lane road	四車線道路み	Yohn-shah-sehn-doh-roh
two-lane road	二車線道路	Nee-shah-sehn-doh-roh
fast lane	追い越し車線	Oh-ee-koh-shee-shah-sehn
left lane	左車線	Hee-dah-ree shah-sehn
right lane	右車線	Mee-gee-shah-sehn
breakdown lane	路肩	Roh-kah-tah

attractions
アトラクション
Ah-toh-rah-koo-shohn

casino
カジノ
Kah-jee-noh

guide book
ガイドブック
Gah-ee-doh book-koo

park
公園
Koh-ehn

guided tour
ガイドツアー
Gah-ee-doh tsoo-ah

information
インフォメーション
Een-foh-meh-shohn

itinerary
日程
Neet-teh-ee

ruins
遺跡
Ee-seh-kee

monument
モニュメント
Moh-nyoo-mehn-toh

museum
博物館
Hah-koo-boo-tsoo-kahn

national park
国立公園
Koh-koo-ree-tsoo-koh-ehn

sightseeing
観光
Kahn-koh

souvenirs
お土産
Oh-mee-yah-geh

tour bus
ツアーバス
Tsoo-ah bah-soo

tourist
旅行者
Ryoh-koh-shah

entrance fee / price	入場料	Nyoo-jyoh-ryoh
to buy a souvenir	お土産を買う	Oh-mee-yah-geh woh kah-oo
to do a tour	ツアーをする	Tsoo-ah woh soo-roo
tour guide	ツアーガイド	Tsoo-ah gah-ee-doh

airport
空港
Koo-koh

bank
銀行
Geen-koh

bus stop
バス停
Bah-soo-teh-ee

church
教会
Kyoh-kah-ee

cinema
映画館
Eh-ee-gah-kahn

city / town hall
市役所
Shee-yah-koo-shoh

department store
デパート
Deh-pah-toh

factory
工場
Koh-jyoh

fire station
消防署
Shoh-boh-shoh

hospital
病院
Byoh-een

hotel
ホテル
Hoh-teh-roo

library
図書館
Toh-shoh-kahn

theatre
劇場
Geh-kee-jyoh

museum
博物館
Hah-koo-boo-tsoo-kahn

parking area
駐車場
Choo-shah-jyoh

playground
遊び場
Ah-soh-bee-bah

police station
警察署
Keh-ee-sah-tsoo-shoh

post office
郵便局
Yoo-been-kyo-koo

prison
刑務所
Keh-moo-shoh

restaurant
レストラン
Reh-soo-toh-rahn

school
学校
Gahk-koh

taxi stand
タクシー乗り場
Tah-koo-shee noh-ree-bah

harbour
港
Mee-nah-toh

square
広場
Hee-roh-bah

supermarket
スーパーマーケット
Soo-pah-mah-keht-toh

railway station
鉄道駅
Teh-tsoo-doh-eh-kee

How do I get to the railway station?	駅へはどうやって行けばいいですか？	Eh-kee eh doh-yaht-teh ee-keh-bah ee-des-kah?
Where can I find a taxi?	どこでタクシーを拾うことが出来ますか？	Doh-koh deh tah-koo-shee woh he-roh-oo koh-toh gah deh-kee-mas-kah?

snorkel
シュノーケル
Shoo-noh-keh-roo

swimming goggles
水中メガネ
Soo-ee-chuh meh-gah-neh

beach ball
ビーチボール
Bee-chee boh-roo

hat
帽子
Boh-shee

diving mask
ゴーグル
Goh-goo-roo

sunscreen
日焼け止めクリーム
Hee-yah-keh-doh-meh koo-ree-moo

beach towel
ビーチタオル
Bee-chee tah-oh-roo

sunglasses
サングラス
Sahn-goo-rah-soo

swimming cap
スイミングキャップ
Soo-ee-meen-gooh kyap-poo

swimming costume
水着
Mee-zoo-gee

beach	ビーチ	Bee-chee
bikini	ビキニ	Bee-kee-nee
sun lounger	屋外用の畳み式ベッド	Yah-gah-ee-yoh tah-tah-mee-shee-kee beht-toh
to sunbathe	日光浴をする	Neek-koh-yoh-koo woh soo-roo
to swim	泳ぐ	Oh-yoh-goo

 HEALTH

medicines
薬
Koo-soo-ree

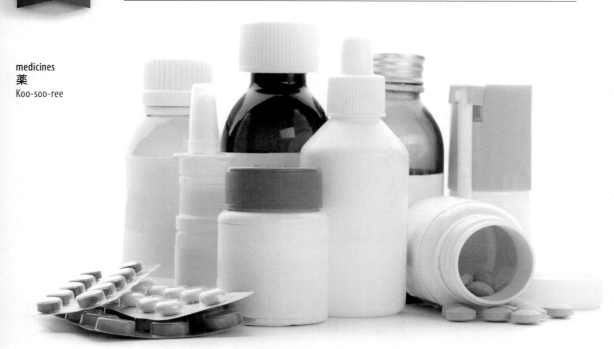

eye drops
目薬
Meh-goo-soo-ree

painkiller
鎮静剤
Cheen-seh-ee-zah-ee

syrup
シロップ
Shee-rohp-poo

to take medicine
薬を飲む
Koo-soo-ree woh noh-moo

shot / injection
注射
Choo-shah

sleeping pill
睡眠薬
Soo-ee-meen-yah-koo

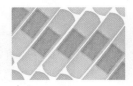
plaster
プラスター
Poo-rah-soo-tah

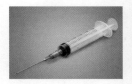
syringe
注射器
Choo-shah-kee

gauze
ガーゼ
Gah-zeh

pill
錠剤
Jyoh-za-ee

tablet
錠剤
Jyoh-za-ee

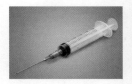
ointment
塗り薬
Noo-ree-goo-soo-ree

hospital
病院
Byoh-eehn

nurse
看護婦
Kahn-goh-foo

doctor / physician
医者
Ee-shah

operation / surgery
手術
Shoo-jyoo-tsoo

patient
患者
Kahn-jah

waiting room
待合室
Mah-chee-ah-ee-shee-tsoo

check-up	検診	Kehn-sah	prescription	処方箋	Shoh-hoh-sehn
diagnosis	診断	sheenh-dahn	specialist	専門家	Sehn-mohn-kah
pharmacy/chemist's	薬局	Yahk-kyoh-koo	treatment	治療法	Chee-ryoh-hoh

allergist
アレルギー専門家
Ah-reh-roo-gee-sehn-mohn-kah

dentist
歯医者
Hah-ee-shah

gynecologist
婦人科医
Foo-jeen-kah-ee

pediatrician
小児科医
Shoh-nee-kah-ee

physiotherapist
理学療法士
Ree-gah-koo-ryo-hoh-shee

midwife
助産師
Jyo-sahn-shee

ophthalmologist
眼科医
Gahn-kah-ee

surgeon
外科医
Gah-ee-kah-ee

anaesthesiologist	麻酔科医	Mah-soo-ee-kah-ee
cardiologist	心臓専門医	Sheen-zoh-sehn-mohn-ee
dermatologist	皮膚科医	Hee-foo-kah-ee
neurologist	神経科医	Sheen-keh-kah-ee
oncologist	腫瘍医	Shoo-yoh-ee
psychiatrist	精神科医	Seh-ee-sheen-kah-ee
radiologist	放射線科医	Hoh-shah-sehn-kah-ee

to feel good
体調がいい
Tah-ee-choh gah ee

to catch a cold
風邪を引く
Kah-zeh woh hee-koo

to have a cold
風邪をひいてる
Kah-zeh woh hee-the-roo

to sneeze
くしゃみ
Koo-shah-mee

to cough
咳をする
Seh-kee woh soo-roo

to blow your nose
鼻をかむ
Hah-nah woh kah-moo

to feel sick
体調が悪い
Tah-ee-choh gah wah-roo-ee

to faint
気絶する
Kee-zeh-tsoo soo-roo

to pass out
倒れる
Tah-oh-reh-roo

to be tired
疲れています
Tsoo-kah-reh-the-ee-mas

to be exhausted
疲れ果てています
Tsoo-kah-reh-hah-the-the-ee-mas

to have back pain
背中が痛い
Seh-nah-kah gah ee-tah-ee

to have earache
耳が痛い
Mee-mee gah ee-tah-ee

to have a headache
頭が痛い
Ah-tah-mah gah ee-tah-ee

to have a sore throat
喉が痛い
Noh-doh gah ee-tah-ee

to have toothache
歯が痛い
Hah gah ee-tah-ee

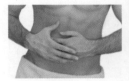

to have a stomach ache
胃が痛い
Ee gah ee-tah-ee

to have a temperature
熱があります
Neh-tsoo gah ah-ree-mah-soo

to have diarrhoea
下痢です
Geh-ree des

to break an arm
腕を骨折する
Oo-deh woh kohs-seh-tsoo
soo-roo

to be constipated
便秘です
Behn-pee des

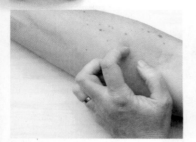

to have a rash
発疹があります
Hash-sheen gah ah-ree-mas

to be allergic to...
。。。にアレルギーを持ってます
... nee ah-roo-reh-gee woh moth-the ee-mas

to vomit
吐く
Hah-koo

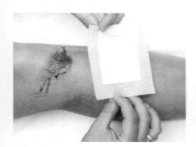

to hurt
怪我する
Keh-gah soo-roo

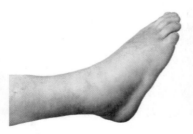

to swell
腫れる
Hah-reh-roo

to suffer from
苦しむ
Koo-roo-shee-moo

chicken pox
水疱瘡
Mee-zoo-boh-soh

runny nose
みずっぱな
Mee-zoo-ppah-nah

cough
咳
Seh-kee

diarrhoea
下痢
Geh-ree

heart attack
心臓発作
Sheen-zoh-hohs-sah

fever
熱
Neh-tsoo

headache
頭痛
Zoo-tsoo

injury
怪我
Keh-gah

sore throat
喉の痛み
Noh-doh noh ee-tah-mee

asthma
喘息
Zehn-zoh-koo

flu
風邪
Lah-zeh

health
健康
Kehn-koh

hepatitis
肝炎
Kahn-ehn

heart disease
心臓病
Sheen-zoh-byoh

stomach ache
腹痛
Foo-koo-tsoo

mouth ulcer
口内炎
Koh-nah-ee-ehn

wound
傷
Kee-zoo

common cold	風邪	Kah-zeh	pain	痛み	Ee-tah-mee
fracture	骨折	Kohs-seh-tsoo	painful	痛い	EE-tah-ee
illness	病	Yah-mah-ee	painless	無痛	Muh-tsoo
mumps	おたふく風邪	Oh-tah-foo-koo kah-zeh	to be ill	病気になる	Byo-kee nee nah-roo

emergency number
緊急番号
Keen-kyoo-bahn-goh

firefighter
消防士
Shoh-boh-shee

policeman
警察官
Keh-ee-sah-tsoo-kahn

fire engine
消防車
Shoh-boh-shah

police car
パトカー
Pah-toh-kah

ambulance
救急車
Kyoo-kyoo-shah

accident
事故
Jee-koh

paramedics
医療補助者
EE-ryo-hoh-jyo-shah

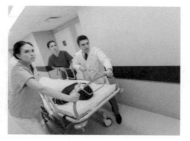

emergency
緊急事態
Keen-kyoo-jee-tah-ee

fire
火事
Kah-jee

patient
患者
Kahn-jya

police
警察
Keh-ee-sah-tsoo

 SPORTS

badminton racket
バドミントンラケット
Bah-doh-mihn-toh

ball
ボール
boh-roo

baseball
野球
Yah-kyoo

bicycle
自転車
Gee-tehn-shah

bowling ball
ボウリングボール
Boh-reehn-goo boh-roo

cap
帽子
Boh-shee

football
サッカーボール
Sahk-kah boh-roo

glove
グローブ
Goo-roh-boo

net
ネット
neht-toh

goggles
ゴーグル
Goh-goo-roo

golf ball
ゴルフボール
Goh-roo-foo boh-roo

helmet
ヘルメット
Heh-roo-meht-toh

goal
ゴール
Goh-roo

hockey puck
ホッケーパック
Hohk-keh pahk-koo

hockey stick
ホッケースティック
Hohk-keh soo-teek-koo

saddle
サドル
Sah-doh-roo

ice-skates
アイススケート
Ah-ee-soo soo-keh-toh

lane
レーン
Reh-ehn

skates
スケート
Soo-keh-toh

ski poles
ストック
Soo-tohk-koo

167

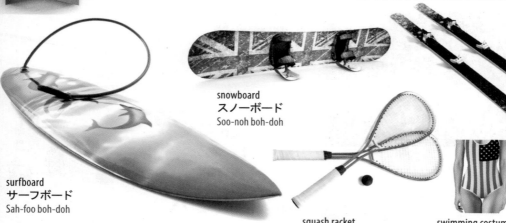

skis
スキー
Soo-kee

snowboard
スノーボード
Soo-noh boh-doh

surfboard
サーフボード
Sah-foo boh-doh

squash racket
スカッシュラケット
Soo-kah-shoo rah-keht-toh

swimming costume
水着
Mee-zoo-gee

tennis ball
テニスボール
Teh-nee-soo boh-roo

tennis racket
テニスラケット
Teh-nee-soo rah-keht-toh

volleyball
バレーボール
Bah-reh-boh-roo

weights
ウエート
Oo-eh-toh

baseball
野球
Yah-kyoo

bowling
ボーリング
Boh-reen-goo

football
サッカー
Sahk-kah

hiking
ハイキング
Hah-ee-keen-goo

hockey
ホッケー
Hohk-keh

cycling
サイクリング
Sah-ee-koo-reen-goo

horseriding
乗馬
Jyoh-bah

running
ランニング
Rahn-neen-goo

skating
スケート
Soo-keh-toh

skiing
スキー
Soo-kee

swimming
水泳
Soo-ee-eh

tennis
テニス
Teh-nee-soo

volleyball
バレーボール
Bah-reh boh-roo

weightlifting
重量挙げ
Jyoo-ryoh ah-geh

basketball court
バスケットボールコート
Bah-soo-keht-toh boh-roo koh-toh

boxing ring
ボクシングリング
Boh-koo-sheen-goo reen-goo

fitness centre
フィットネスセンター
Feey-toh-neh-soo sehn-tah

football pitch
サッカー場
Sahk-kah Joh

golf course
ゴルフコース
Goh-roo-foo koh-soo

football ground
サッカー場
Sahk-kah jyoh

golf club
ゴルフ場
Goh-roo-foo jyoh

gym
ジム
Gee-moo

playground
遊び場
Ah-soh-bee bah

racecourse
レースコース
Reh-soo Koh-toh

race track
レーストラック
Reh-soo toh-rahk-koo

recreation area
レクリエーションエリア
Reh-koo-reh-shohn Eh-ree-ah

skating rink
スケートリンク
Soo-keh-toh reen-koo

sports ground
スポーツグラウンド
Soo-poh-tsoo goo-rahn-doh

stadium
スタジアム
Soo-tah-gee-ah-moo

swimming pool
プール
Poo-roo

tennis club
テニスクラブ
Teh-nee-soo koo-rah-boo

tennis court
テニスコート
Teh-nee-soo koh-toh

NATURE

landscape
風景
Foo-keh-ee

bay
湾
Wahn

beach
ビーチ
Bee-chee

cave
洞窟
Doh-koo-tsoo

creek
入り江
Ee-ree-eh

desert
砂漠
Sah-bah-koo

forest   woods
森林   森
Sheen-reen   Moh-ree

hill
丘
Oh-kah

earth
地球
Chee-kyoo

island
島
Shee-mah

lake
湖
Mezoo-oo-mee

mountain
山
Yah-mah

ocean
海洋
Kah-ee-oh

peak
頂上
Choh-jyoh

plain
平原
Heh-ee-gehn

pond
池
Ee-keh

river
川
Kah-wah

sea
海
Oo-mee

stream
小川
Oh-gah-wah

swamp
沼
Noo-mah

valley
谷
Tah-nee

waterfall
滝
Tah-kee

weather
天気
Tehn-kee

| What's the weather like? | 天気はどうですか。 | Tehn-kee wah doh-des-kah |
| What's the forecast for tomorrow? | 明日の天気情報はどうですか。 | Ah-shee-tah noh tehn-kee Jyoh-hoh wah doh-des-kah |

blizzard
吹雪
Foo-boo-kee

cold
寒気
Kahn-kee

drizzle
小雨
Koh-sah-meh

flood
洪水
Koh-zoo-ee

frost
霜
Shee-moh

humidity
湿気
Sheek-keh

Celsius
セルシウス
Seh-roo-shee-oo-soo

cyclone
低気圧
The-kee-ah-tsoo

dry
乾燥
Kahn-soh

fog
霧
Kee-ree

hail
氷雨
Hee-sah-meh

hurricane
ハリケーン
Hah-ree-kehn

cloud
雲
Koo-moh

degree
温度
Ohn-doh

dry season
乾季
Kahn-kee

forecast
予想
Yoh-soh

heat
熱さ
Ah-tsoo-sah

ice
氷
Koh-ree

cloudy
曇り
Koo-moh-ree

dew
梅雨
Tsoo-yoo

Fahrenheit
華氏
Kah-shee

freeze
氷点下
Hyo-tehn-kah

hot
暑い
Ah-tsoo-ee

lightning
稲妻
Ee-nah-zoo-mah

rain
雨
Ah-meh

rainy season
雨季
Oo-kee

snowy
雪深い
Yoo-kee-boo-kah-ee

temperature
温度
Ohn-doh

tsunami
津波
Tsoo-nah-mee

rainstorm
暴風雨
Boh-foo-oo

sleet
凍雨
Toh-oo

storm
嵐
Ah-rah-shee

thunder
カミナリ
Kah-mee-nah-ree

typhoon
台風
Tah-ee-foo

windy
風が強い
Kah-zeh gah tsoo-yoh-ee

rainbow
虹
Nee-jee

snow
雪
Yoo-kee

sun
太陽
Tah-ee-yoh

thunderstorm
雷雨
Rah-ee-oo

warm
暖かい
Ah-tah-tah-kah-ee

rainy
雨が降ってる
Ah-meh gah foo-tte-roo

snowstorm
雪嵐
Yoo-kee-ah-rah-shee

sunny
晴れ
Hah-reh

tornado
竜巻
Tah-tsoo-mah-kee

wind
風
Kah-zeh

pet owner
飼い主
Kah-ee-noo-shee

aquarium
水槽
Soo-ee-soh

cage
檻
Oh-ree

canary
カナリヤ
Kah-nah-ree-ah

bird
鳥
Toh-ree

dog
犬
Ee-noo

cat
猫
Neh-koh

pet shop
ペットショップ
Peht-toh-shohp-poo

fish
金魚
Keen-gyoh

gecko
ヤモリ
Yah-moh-ree

hamster
ハムスター
Hah-moo-soo-tah

guinea pig
ギニーピッグ
Gee-nee-peeg-goo

lizard
トカゲ
Toh-kah-geh

rabbit
ウサギ
Oo-sah-gee

rat
ネズミ
Neh-soo-mee

mouse
ネズミ
Neh-zoo-mee

parrot
オウム
Oh-oo-moo

snake
蛇
Heh-bee

spider
クモ
Koo-moh

cow
牛
Oo-shee

chicken
鶏
Nee-wah-toh-ree

donkey
ロバ
Roh-bah

goose
ガチョウ
Gah-choh

goat
ヤギ
Yah-gee

horse
馬
Oo-mah

sheep
羊
Hee-tsoo-jee

duck
鴨
Kah-moh

rabbit
ウサギ
Oo-sah-gee

pig
豚
Boo-tah

turkey
七面鳥
Shee-chee-mehn-choh

giraffe
キリン
Kee-reen

elephant
像
Zoh-oo

jaguar
ジャガー
Jya-gah

tiger
トラ
Toh-rah

lion
ライオン
Rah-ee-ohn

leopard
ヒョウ
Hyoh

puma
プーマ
Poo-mah

hippopotamus
カバ
Kah-bah

monkey
猿
Sah-roo

chimpanzee
チンパンジー
Cheen-pahn-jee

ostrich
ダチョウ
Dah-choh

rhinoceros
サイ
Sah-ee

armadillo
アルマジロ
Ah-roo-mah-jee-roh

sloth
ナマケモノ
Nah-mah-keh-moh-noh

iguana
イグアナ
Ee-goo-ah-nah

kangaroo
カンガルー
Kahn-gah-roo

bear
熊
Koo-mah

zebra
ゼブラ
Zeh-boo-rah

hyena
ハイエナ
Hah-ee-eh-nah

seal
アザラシ
Ah-zah-rah-shee

gazelle
ガゼル
Gah-zeh-roo

antelope
カモシカ
Kah-moh-shee-kah

python
ニシキヘビ
Nee-shee-kee-heh-bee

water buffalo
水牛
Soo-ee-gyoo

boar
いのしし
Ee-noh-noh-shee-shee

cobra
コブラ
Koh-boo-rah

whale
クジラ
Koo-jee-rah

killer whale
シャチ
Shah-chee

shark
サメ
Sah-meh

turtle
亀
Kah-meh

dolphin
イルカ
Ee-roo-kah

crocodile
ワニ
Wah-nee

11 🛒

SHOPPING AND SERVICES

food market
食料市場
Shoh-koo-ryoh Ee-chee-bah

bazaar
バザール
Bah-zah-roo

bookshop
本屋
Hohn=yah

computer shop
コンピューターショップ
Kohn-pyoo-tah-shohp-poo

corner shop
街角の雑貨屋
Mah-chee-kah-doh noh
Zahk-kah-yah

farmers' market
農産用マーケット
Noh-sahn-toh-mah-keht-toh

flea market
フリーマーケット
Foo-ree-mah-keht-toh

flower market
花屋
Hah-nah-yah

bakery
パン屋
Pahn-yah

fruit stall
果物屋
Koo-dah-moh-noh-yah

market
市場
Ee-chee-bah

newsagent
新聞屋
Sheen-boon-yah

shoe shop
靴屋
Koo-tsoo-yah

street vendor
露天商
Roh-tehn-shoh

supermarket
スーパーマーケット
Soo-pah-mah-keht-toh

department store	デパート	Deh-pah-toh
grocery store	食料品店	Shoh-koo-ryoh-heen-tehn
shopping centre	ショッピングセンター	Sohp-peen-goo-sehn-tah

sale
特売
Toh-koo-bah-ee

checkout / till checkout
勘定
Kahn-jyo

conveyor belt
ベルトコンベアー
Beh-roo-toh kohn-beh-ah

customer
客
Kya-koo

price
値段
Neh-dahn

queue
列
Reh-tsoo

receipt
レシート
Reh-shee-toh

cashier
レジ
Reh-jee

shopping bag
買い物袋
Kah-ee-moh-noh-boo-koo-roh

shopping list
買い物リスト
Kah-ee-moh-noh ree-soo-toh

shopping basket
買い物かご
Kah-ee-moh-noh-kah-goh

trolley
カート
Kah-toh

bill for	請求書	Seh-kyoo-shoh
Can I help you?	なにか手伝いましょうか、	Nah-nee-kah the-tsoo-dah-ee-mah-shoh-kah
goods	グッズ	Good-zoo
shopper	買い物客	Kah-ee-moh-noh kya-koo
to cost	コストをかける	Koh-soo-toh woh kah-keh-roo
to get a great bargain	大バーゲン	Dah-ee-bah-gehn
to purchase	購入する	Koh-nyuu-soo-roo
to queue	列に並ぶ	Reh-tsoo nee nah-rah-boo

belt
ベルト
Beh-roo-toh

boots
ブーツ
Boo-tsoo

coat
コート
Koh-toh

raincoat
レインコート
Reh-een-koh-toh

gloves
手袋
The-boo-koo-roh

hat
帽子
Boh-shee

jeans
ジーンズ
Jeen-zoo

pyjamas
パジャマ
Pah-jya-mah

jacket
ジャケット
Jya-keht-toh

shoes
靴
Koo-tsoo

jumper
ジャンパー
Jyan-pah

scarf
スカーフ
Soo-kah-foo

underwear
下着
Shee-tah-gee

tie
ネクタイ
Neh-koo-tah-ee

briefs
ブリーフ
Boo-ree-foo

shirt
シャツ
Shah-tsoo

sweatshirt
トレーナー
Toh-reh-nah

suit
スーツ
Soo-tsoo

t-shirt
Tシャツ
Tee-shah-tsoo

undershirt
アンダーシャツ
Ahn-dah shah-tsoo

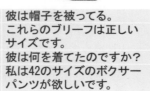

socks
靴下
Koo-tsoo-shee-tah

slippers
スリッパ
Soo-reep-pah

trousers
ズボン
Zoo-bohn

He has a hat on.	彼は帽子を被ってる。	Kah-reh wah boh-shee woh kah-boot-the-roo
These briefs are the right size.	これらのブリーフは正しいサイズです。	Koh-reh-rah noh boo-re-foo wah tah-dah-shee sah-ee-zoo des
What did he have on?	彼は何を着てたのですか？	Kah-reh wah nah-nee woh kee-the-tah noh des-kah
I want these boxer shorts in a size 42.	私は42のサイズのボクサーパンツが欲しいです。	Wah-tah-shee wah Yohn-jyoo-nee noh sah-ee-zoo noh boh-koo-sah pahn-tsoo gah hoh-shee des

jacket
ジャケット
Jya-keht-toh

boots
ブーツ
Boo-tsoo

gloves
手袋
The-boo-koo-roh

raincoat
レインコート
Reh-een-koh-toh

coat
コート
Koh-toh

hat
帽子
Boh-shee

jeans
ジーンズ
Jeen-zoo

pyjamas
パジャマ
Pah-jya-mah

belt
ベルト
Beh-roo-toh

dress
ドレス
Doh-reh-soo

scarf
スカーフ
Soo-kah-foo

jumper
ジャンパー
Jyan-pah

pants
パンツ
Pahn-tsoo

skirt
スカート
Soo-kah-toh

shoes
靴
Koo-tsoo

sweatshirt
トレーナー
Toh-reh-nah

socks
靴下
Koo-tsoo-shee-tah

shirt
シャツ
Shah-tsoo

stockings
ストッキング
Soo-toh-keen-goo

t-shirt
Tシャツ
Tee-shah-tsoo

suit
スーツ
Soo-tsoo

underwear
下着
Shee-tah-gee

trousers
ズボン
Zoo-bohn

slacks
スラックス
Soo-rahk-koo-soo

bra
ブラジャー
Boo-rah-jya

slippers
スリッパ
Soo-reep-pah

She has a hat on.	彼女は帽子を被ってる。	Kah-noh-jyo wah boh-shee woh kah-boot-teh-roo
The dress looks nice on you.	そのドレスはあなたに似合っている。	Soh-noh doh-reh-soo ha ah-nah-tah nee nee-aht-teh-roo
What did she have on?	彼女は何を着てたのですか？	Kah-noh-jyo wah nah-nee woh kee-teh-tah noh des-kah?
I want these boots in a size 38.	私は38のサイズのブーツが欲しいです。	Wah-tah-shee wah Sahn-jyoo-hah-chee noh sah-ee-zoo boo-tsoo gah hoh-shee des.

barber shop
床屋
Toh-koh-yah

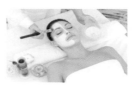

beauty salon
ビューティーサロン
Byoo-tee sah-rohn

bicycle repair shop
自転車修理屋
Jee-tehn-sha shoo-ree-yah

watchmaker
時計屋
Toh-keh-ee-yah

car repair shop
自動車修理店
Jee-doh-sha shoo-ree-tehn

laundromat
コインランドリー
Koh-een rahn-doh-ree

dry-cleaning
ドライクリーニング
Doh-rah-ee-koo-ree-neen-goo

locksmith's shop
鍵屋
Kah-gee-yah

petrol station
ガソリンスタンド
Gah-soh-reen soo-than-doh

CULTURE AND MEDIA

blog
ブログ
Boo-roh-goo

to broadcast
放送
Hoh-oo-soh

magazine
雑誌
Zahs-shee

newspaper
新聞
Sheen-boon

radio
ラジオ
Rah-jee-oh

television
テレビ
The-reh-bee

news broadcast
ニュース番組
Nyoo-soo bahn-goo-mee

weather forecast
天気予報
Tehn-kee-yoh-hoh

blogosphere	ブロゴスフィア	Boo-roh-goo-soo-fee-ah
mass media	マスメディア	Mah-soo-meh-dee-ah
news	ニュース	Nyoo-soo
press	マスコミ	Mah-soo-koh-mee
tabloid	タブロイド	Tah-boo-roh-ee-doh
programme	番組	Bahn-goo-mee
soap	ドラマ	Doh-rah-mah
drama	ドラマ	Doh-rah-mah
series	シリーズ	Shee-ree-soo
film	映画	Eh-ee-gah
documentary	ドキュメンタリー	Doh-kyoo-mehn-tah-ree
music programme	音楽番組	Ohn-gah-koo-bahn-goo-mee
sports programme	スポーツ番組	Soo-poh-tsoo-bahn-goo-mee
talk show	トークショー	Toh-koo-shoh
episode	エピソード	Eh-pee-soh-doh
business news	ビジネスニュース	Bee-jee-neh-soo-nyoo-soo
sports report	スポーツレポート	Soo-poh-tsoo-reh-poh-toh
book review	書評	Jee-hyoh
ad / advertisement	広告	Koh-koh-koo

message
メッセージ
Mehs-seh-jee

address / URL
URLアドレス
Yoo-ah-roo-eh-roo ah-doh-reh-soo

application / app
アプリ
Ah-poo-ree

network
ネットワーク
Neht-toh-wah-koo

inbox	受信箱	Jyoo-sheen-bah-koh
IP address	IPアドレス	Ah-ee-pee Ah-doh-reh-soo
internet	インターネット	Een-tah-neht-toh
website	ウェブサイト	Weh-boo-sah-ee-toh
mail	メール	Meh-roo
search engine	検索エンジン	Kehn-sah-koo-ehn-jeen
to search	検索する	Kehn-sah-koo soo-roo
to share	シェアする	Sheh-ah soo-roo
to log in	ログインする	Roh-goo-een

to send
送信する
Soh-sheen soo-roo

login
ログイン
Roh-goo-een soo-roo

to log out
ログアウトする
Roh-goo-ah-oo-toh soo-roo

to upload	アップロードする	Ahp-poo roh-doh soo-roo
to download	ダウンロードする	Dah-oon-roh-doh soo-roo
to tag	タグをつける	Tah-goo woh tsoo-keh-roo
to comment	コメントする	Koh-mehn-toh soo-roo
to publish	表記する	Hyoh-kee soo-roo
to contact	コンタクトをとる	Kohn-tah-koo-toh woh toh-roo
to receive	受信	Jyoo-sheen
to add	追加する	Tsoo-ee-kah

link
リンク
Reen-koo

CD
シーディ
Shee-dee

CD-ROM
シーディーロム
Shee-dee-roh-moo

DVD
ディービーディ
Dee-bee-dee

mouse
マウス
Ma-oo-soo

keyboard
キーボード
Kee-boh-doh

USB flash drive
USBメモリー
Yoo-eh-soo-bee-
meh-moh-ree

laptop
ノートパソコン
Noh-toh-pah-soh-kohn

modem
モデム
Moh-deh-moo

monitor
モニター
Moh-nee-tah

router
ルーター
Roo-tah

tablet
タブレット
Tah-boo-reht-toh

printer
印刷機
Een-sah-tsoo-kee

scanner
スキャナー
Soo-kya-nah

to copy	コピーをとる	Koh-pee woh toh-roo		to print	印刷する	Een-sah-tsoo soo-roo
to delete	削除する	Hah-ee-jyoh soo-roo		to save	保存する	Hoh-zohn soo-roo
desktop	デスクトップ	Deh-soo-koo-tohp-poo		to scan	スキャンをとる	Soo-kyan woh toh-roo
file	ファイル	Fah-ee-roo		screenshot	スクリーンショット	Soo-koo-reen-shoht-toh
folder	フォルダー	Foh-roo-dah		server	サーバー	Sah-bah
offline	オフライン	Oh-foo-rah-een		software	ソフトウエア	Soh-foo-toh-oo-eh-ah
online	オンライン	Ohn-rah-een		to undo	元に戻す	Moh-toh nee moh-doh-soo
password	パスワード	Pah-soo-wah-doh		virus	ウイルス	Oo-ee-roo-soo

at
アットマーク
Aht-toh-mah-koo

hash
ハッシュ
Has-shoo

percent
パーセント
Pah-sehn-toh

circumflex
シルコンフレックス
Shee-roo-kohn-foo-rehk-koo-soo

ampersand
アンド
Ahn-doh

asterisk
アステリスク
Ah-soo-the-reek-koo-soo

tilde
チルダ
Chee-roo-dah

tab key
タブキー
Tah-boo-kee

caps lock key
キャプスロックキー
Kya-poo-soo-rohk-koo-kee

shift key
シフトキー
Shee-foo-toh-kee

ctrl (control) key
コントロールキー
Kohn-toh-roh-roo-kee

WIRELESS KEYBOARD K900

Esc   F1   F2   F3   F4   F5   F6   F7   F8   F9   F10

~ `   ! 1   @ 2   # 3 $ 4   % 5   ^ 6   & 7   * 8   (9

Tab   Q W E R T Y U I O

Caps Lock   A S D F G H J K L

Shift   Z X C V B N M < ,

Ctrl   Fn   Start   Alt   Alt Gr

exclamation mark
びっくりマーク
Beek-koo-ree-mah-koo

alt (alternate) key
アルトキー
Ah-roo-toh-kee

spacebar key
スペースキー
Soo-peh-soo-kee

minus / dash
マイナスキー
Mah-ee-nah-soo-kee

plus
プラスキー
Poo-rah-soo-kee

equal
イコール
Ee-koh-roo

colon
重点
Joo-tehn

semicolon
セミコロン
Seh-mee-koh-rohn

dot / full stop
ドット
Doht-toh

question mark
クエッションマーク
Koo-ehs-shohn-mah-koo

enter key
入力キー
Nyoo-ryoh-koo-kee

forward slash
スラッシュ
Soo-rahs-shoo

back slash
バックスラッシュ
Bahk-koo-soo-rahs-shoo

backspace key
バックスペースキー
Bahk-koo-soo-peh-soo-kee

delete or del key
デリートキー
Deh-ree-toh-kee

amusement park
遊園地
Yoo-ehn-chee

aquarium
水族館
Soo-ee-zoh-koo-kahn

art gallery
アートギャラリー
Ah-toh-gyah-rah-ree

art museum
美術館
Bee-jyoo-tsoo-kahn

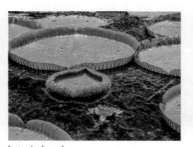

botanical garden
植物園
Shoh-koo-boo-tsoo-ehn

cinema
映画館
Eh-gah-kahn

circus
サーカス
Sah-kah-soo

discotheque
ディスコ
Dee-soo-koh

garden
お庭
Oh-nee-wah

night club
ナイトクラブ
Nah-ee-toh-koo-rah-boo

trade fair / trade show
公益会
Koh-eh-kee-kah-ee

opera house
オペラハウス
Oh-peh-rah-hah-oo-soo

concert hall
コンサートホール
Kohn-sah-toh-hoh-roo

park
公園
Koh-ehn

planetarium
プラネタリウム
Poo-rah-neh-tah-ree-oo-moo

science museum
科学博物館
Kah-gah-koo-hah-koo-boo-tsoo-kahn

sights
観光
Kahn-koh

theatre
劇場
Geh-kee-jyoh

tourist attraction
観光アトラクション
Kahn-koh-ahtoh-rah-koo-shohn

water park
ウォーターパーク
Woh-tah-pah-koo

zoo
動物園
Doh-boo-tsoo-ehn

accordion
アコーディオン
Ah-koh-dee-ohn

bagpipes
バグパイプ
Bah-goo-pah-ee-poo

castanets
カスタネット
Kah-soo-tah-neht-toh

cello
チェロ
Cheh-roh

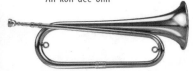

bugle
ラッパ
Rahp-pah

banjo
バンジョー
Bahn-jyo

clarinet
クラリネット
Koo-rah-ree-neht-toh

cymbals
シンバル
Sheen-bah-roo

drum
ドラム
Doh-rah-moo

electric guitar
エレキギター
Eh-reh-kee-gee-tah

drum set
ドラムセット
Doh-rah-moo seht-toh

flute
フルート
Foo-roo-toh

harmonica
ハーモニカ
Hah-moh-nee-kah

guitar
ギター
Gee-tah

grand piano
グランドピアノ
Goo-rahn-doh-pee-ah-noh

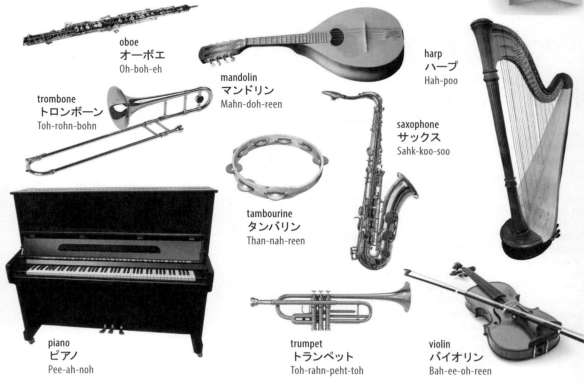

oboe
オーボエ
Oh-boh-eh

mandolin
マンドリン
Mahn-doh-reen

harp
ハープ
Hah-poo

trombone
トロンボーン
Toh-rohn-bohn

saxophone
サックス
Sahk-koo-soo

tambourine
タンバリン
Than-nah-reen

piano
ピアノ
Pee-ah-noh

trumpet
トランペット
Toh-rahn-peht-toh

violin
バイオリン
Bah-ee-oh-reen

Index

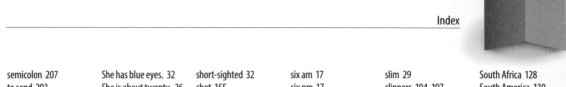